ENDORSEMENTS

"Paul Becker recounts his adventures in a clear, entertaining, and relevant style that's incredibly enjoyable to read. With his grounded and engaging writing style, Paul's story is appealing for any reader, regardless of age or religious affiliation. I felt my own strength as a Christian grow and develop as he told his story, and I highly recommend this book for any young person looking to get more involved with their faith and sharing the Good News with others."

— Hannah L. Cox, College Student

"This book is a huge encouragement to step out into a more lively, adventurous life with a perfectly loving and sovereign God! I feel driven to take refuge in the Word of God and the plans he has for me because I know his path for me is far greater than any of my expectations. This book provides great practical steps on how to follow the path he has set out for you, which will prepare young adults to be great leaders and representatives of the Lord!"

— Talia Standley, College Student

"Dr. Paul Becker opens up about his younger years in a vulnerable and humble way. Through life learning adventures as an agnostic, he beautifully paints a picture of how God was protecting, revealing, and calling him into a personal relationship. Please read this entire book and learn the importance of prayer and consulting God before making any important decisions in life. There are thought-provoking reflection questions at the end of every chapter that will help you persevere and live out the calling God has for your precious life."

— Rev. Jeffrey Smith
DCPI International NexGen Director

WALK
ON THE
WILD SIDE
WITH GOD

WALK ON THE WILD SIDE WITH GOD

Facing Death, God, and a Faith-Filled Future

PAUL BECKER AND AMY BAYER

ILLUSTRATIONS BY LINDSEY HORNKOHL

DCPI DYNAMIC CHURCH PLANTING INTERNATIONAL

WALK ON THE WILD SIDE WITH GOD

Published by Equip Press, Colorado Springs, CO

Scripture quotations marked (NIV) are taken from the Holy Bible, New International Version. Copyright © 1973, 1978, 1984, 2011 by Biblica, Inc.® Used by permission. All rights reserved worldwide.

Scripture quotations marked (NRSV) are taken from the New Revised Standard Version Bible, copyright © 1989 the Division of Christian Education of the National Council of the Churches of Christ in the United States of America. Used by permission. All rights reserved.

First Edition: 2021
Walk on the Wild Side with God / Paul Becker and Amy Bayer
Paperback ISBN: 978-1-951304-64-5
eBook ISBN: 978-1-951304-65-2

DEDICATION

I, Paul, would like to dedicate this book to my…

Wife, Cathy, for being my amazing life and mission partner and the love of my life!

Daughter, Jessica, for her life of love for babies, children, and their parents!

Son, Brandon, for being a superb dad and for his quest with God to equip leaders worldwide using online training.

Daughter-in-love, Jennifer, for being a marvelous mom and leading Christians into the presence of the Most High God.

I would especially like to dedicate this book to our grandchildren, whose walk on the wild side of God is just beginning:

Lynnlee, age five, for the way she loves people and has a great plan for their lives.

Joshua Paul, age three, for the way he makes angels in the sand wearing just his shorts on the beach in San Diego during the winter. Pure joy!

To young leaders in their teens and twenties who choose to have a wild lifetime of adventure with God.

And to the young at heart of any age, who make the choice to leave behind a "safe" existence, overcome fear, and get up and go!

Walk on the Wild Side of Faith in God and see him do miracles in your lives!

I, Amy, would like to dedicate this book to my...

Husband, Scott. Thank you for your support and belief in me. Thank you for being a man who believes in the power of women. I love how you never shy back from taking bold steps forward in your life. Go get 'em, babe!

Children—Luke, Arwen, Abigail, and Teagan. May you enjoy God exceedingly as you step out in faith and follow him wherever he leads. May every adventure of your lives be filled to overflowing with God's blessing, presence, and anointing.

CONTENTS

THE BEST DAY OF MY LIFE

Amy Bayer

A few years ago, as a young twenty-something, I had the honor of taking a two-week trip with DCPI to Kenya, where I had what I affectionately refer to as "the best day of my life." Since that day, I have gotten married and given birth to four beautiful children, and, of course, those are the best days of my life, but the day I spent with Paul Becker and his wife, Cathy, in Maasai Mara, Kenya, will forever be among my most memorable and wonderful days. That's where I found myself dumbfounded at the glory of God. I experienced something so uniquely different from anything else I'd ever seen or done before that my perception of God and his creation shifted.

We stayed in a safari lodge tent camp, where the wake-up call was a delivery of hot tea and coffee alongside small ginger cookies in a bowl on a petite table. In my sleepiness, I told Juliet, the staff member bringing my tea, "Just leave it outside the tent. I'll be up in a minute."

Juliet kindly replied in her singsongy tone, "Oh, I can't, Miss Amy. The monkeys will get it." She unzipped my tent and let herself in, placing the small table to the side of my bed. "Did you sleep like a baby?"

I was about to reply when I heard the scampering of small monkey feet across the roof of my tent and the snuffling of a warthog at the bottom of the steps. I knew this was going to be one of the best days of my life.

Outside, I greeted Paul, Cathy, and the rest of our group as we climbed into the stadium-seated vehicle and headed toward the reserve. The icy morning air cut through my fleece, invigorating the sleepiness out of my body. We rolled and bounced onto dirt trails as we caught our first glimpse of giraffes and zebras walking about in the dawning light.

We spent the morning hours pursuing hyenas, wildebeest, ostriches, elephants, hippos, waterbuck, meerkats, and a whole swath of deerlike creatures prancing across the savanna. The birds tweeted their morning greeting as we pulled our jeep under an umbrella-shaped tree and set up breakfast. After a gorgeous spread of warm eggs, potatoes, and delicious African delicacies, we mounted up again for the continuation of one of the best days of my life.

We spent the day watching and photographing baby elephants, cheetah chases, and lions eating carcasses. We watched for the illustrious Big Five animals and saw all but rhinoceroses. I could not keep my mouth quiet as the sun faded from overhead toward the encircling mountain range and began to set. "Wow! Wow! Wow. Wow, God!"

Together, our team worshipped the Maker of all this exquisite beauty.

We capped off the day back at camp with a delicious dinner under the stars followed by a traditional Maasai warrior jumping ceremony. I stood enamored at all the newness of the day's experiences.

As I curled into my bed that night with a cozy hot-water bottle warming my toes, I whispered, "Thank you, God, for providing for me to be here today. You truly are a wonderful Maker."

The best day of my life poured over into the following days, and I was sad to leave Maasai Mara when the time came. As we gathered our possessions and prepared to board our dirt-runway airplane flight back to Nairobi, I got one last surprise. Jackson, one of our guides, looked at Cathy and said, "I'll give you fifteen cows for her!" I knew this was a proposal of marriage. What a trip! Now I could say I had seen a cheetah and a leopard, and I'd been offered marriage.

Cathy replied to Jackson, "Ha! Try one thousand!"

To which Jackson stated, "Fifteen is the most anybody ever gets."

I smiled and made eye contact as if to say, "Thank you for the offer," as I turned and boarded our small airplane.

Before this wild adventure with God, I had been overwhelmed and intimidated about making the trip around the world, and I almost didn't go. But I'm so glad I did! Adventuring with God can be scary, but the memories you tuck away in your heart are like rare and precious gems that are yours to keep forever. I will never forget the way the light silhouetted the acacia trees in the evening, the way the giraffe's legs folded inward as he walked, the way elephant herds cared for their little pink babies, the way the breeze swept across the grasses and into our wonder-filled faces, and the way God's majesty hovered over the savanna and our team sang "How Great Is Our God" about his gorgeous creation.

It sounds strange to say it this way, but all I wanted to do when I got back home was go to the zoo and watch the movie *The Lion King* because that was the closest I could get to anything like Maasai Mara. It was as if I had never experienced this flavor of God's glory before, and I wanted more.

When you step out in faith and go somewhere new, you get to see a different side of the God you thought you already knew. By saying yes to a God adventure, you're essentially saying, "Open my eyes. I'm ready to see more of who you are."

Since that day, I've had a number of wild adventures with Paul and Cathy Becker, and each time I worship God in a new way.

So, if you're ever afraid to take a walk on the wild side with God, remember: *beautiful treasure awaits you if you're willing to say yes.*

THE CALL
TO LIVE WILDLY

Paul Becker

As a young person, I loved adventure. I was ready to go, to see, and to encounter a world of unknown places, unfamiliar people, and even uncomfortable experiences. I wanted to take it all in. I wanted to see for myself everything I had read about and watched on television as a kid. I wanted to dive deep, climb high, and feel the sweat of hard work on my brow as I explored every new dimension of this vast earth. You see, I grew up in a suburb of Minneapolis, Minnesota, in the United States, and my childhood was safe, structured, and secure. My parents gave me many wonderful opportunities as a child, but life was predictable, and I couldn't help but feel a fire inside of me, a burning desire to take risks, fulfill dreams, and truly live!

So, I set out at the age of eighteen to a university called New College in Sarasota, Florida. This school was designed to let students learn through experiences, and, as you'll read in the chapters of this book, I chose some truly wild experiences. But what I didn't know was that, as I encountered the marvelous world that God made, I would be unable to escape his goodness, his power, and his love for me. Though for most of my teenage years I considered myself agnostic, as I adventured, the sights, sounds, and people of this wild world echoed through the corridors of my mind, inviting me to ask questions about how any of this could possibly be an accident.

I began to realize that what I loved about adventure was the unexpectedness of what I would encounter. And, I began to realize that faith in God was actually the best kind of adventure.

Second Corinthians 5:7 says, "For we live by faith, not by sight."

The wild risk of cave diving and the insane rush of cliff jumping are nothing compared to the exhilaration of giving your life to a God who has a good plan, who has mapped out every continent of this world and every moment of your life. So, as you'll read in this book, I eventually decided to live by faith and not by sight, and wow, has it been a wild ride!

When I gave my life to Jesus, boring life dissolved into vivid living. I didn't have to plan out a future of security and safety for myself; I got to surrender my fears into the big hands of a God who holds the universe, and that meant I no longer had to worry about seeing every step of my journey laid out before me. I got to step forward one season, one adventure at a time. If God said go, I could go. If God said speak, I could speak. If God said sit, I could sit. If God said uproot, I could uproot.

For those of you who are like me, the idea of living by faith and not by sight can be wonderfully exciting. For those of you who are less inclined toward risk-taking, the idea of following God step by step can be overwhelmingly intimidating. What if I don't have what I need? What if my parents disapprove? What if I miss out on a better opportunity? What if my adventure fails miserably?

For some, the idea of life as a faith adventure can stir up images of jumping with Maasai warriors around a Kenyan campfire, dancing colorfully in an Indian sari, or marching up mountains to tell the Good

News about Jesus. It can bring up feelings of being like Indiana Jones, exploring mysterious caves and seeing wonders hidden for centuries. But for others, the idea of life as a faith adventure can bring up hesitations. Like, *what if God leads me to a miserable island with dirty water and strange people to talk to?* Life as a faith adventure may sound like a one-way ticket to a life of mission work in Timbuktu with no contact with the modern world and even less contact with the people you love.

But here's the good news:

Psalm 139:1–4

¹ *You have searched me, Lord,*
  and you know me.
² *You know when I sit and when I rise;*
  you perceive my thoughts from afar.
³ *You discern my going out and my lying down;*
  you are familiar with all my ways.
⁴ *Before a word is on my tongue*
  you, Lord, know it completely.

God made you and knows your unique bent. He understands every concern you have. God is so clued in to your thinking that he knows what you're going to say before you say it! God is wildly in love with you.

Psalm 139:7–10

⁷ *Where can I go from your Spirit?*
  Where can I flee from your presence?
⁸ *If I go up to the heavens, you are there;*
  if I make my bed in the depths, you are there.
⁹ *If I rise on the wings of the dawn,*
  if I settle on the far side of the sea,
¹⁰ *even there your hand will guide me,*
  your right hand will hold me fast.

There is not a place in this entire world where you could get away from God's presence.

Psalm 139:13–16

¹³ *For you created my inmost being;*
   you knit me together in my mother's womb.
¹⁴ *I praise you because I am fearfully and wonderfully made;*
   your works are wonderful,
   I know that full well.
¹⁵ *My frame was not hidden from you*
   when I was made in the secret place,
   when I was woven together in the depths of the earth.
¹⁶ *Your eyes saw my unformed body;*
   all the days ordained for me were written in your book
   before one of them came to be.

He made you wonderfully, and there is no mistake in how God designed you and who he created you to be. God thinks about you all the time. Every day when you wake up, he is still there. He still loves you.

For those who are fearful, know this: God has a unique adventure designed for you based on who he made you to be. Choosing to live by faith and not by sight doesn't mean giving up who you are! It means laying your life down before a God who already likes who you are. His perfect plan for your life weaves together all the cords of your passions with your past experiences, your spiritual gifts, and your unique skills for your joy and his glory! For some, God's plan may be wilder than it is for others, but the only essential ingredient is your faith. As you choose to believe God for a great and wonderful adventure in your life and trust him when he says to go, or to speak, or to wait, or to be silent, you'll see that his plans for you are good, and wild, and fun, and full of life because he's in them.

There is no such thing as a failed adventure with God. Every adventure comes with layers of meaning and life-change when you serve a God who is carefully writing your story for your good and his glory. There's no such thing as missing out on a better opportunity because God is the door opener and the door closer, and he can open better doors than you ever imagined if you trust him.

He is the never-changing, ever-faithful, all-knowing, and unimaginably kind God, and his call for his people to walk by faith is an invitation for them to live a life of adventure, turning every new and unexpected corner with great anticipation.

As you read my story of following God through all the adventures he had planned for me in my late teens and early twenties, think about your life and the ministry adventures he is placing before you. I wrote this book to share some of the stories of crazy-wild things I have experienced and what I learned through them. My hope is that these pages will open your eyes and excite you about the kind of life you can have as you follow God.

You'll hear about my adventures scuba diving in a cave in Florida, being mentored by the wildest adventurer I'd ever met, sailing around one of the Virgin Islands by myself, living on a kibbutz in Israel, canoeing with the gators in the Florida Everglades, hiking in the Mica Basin, rappelling and belaying throughout Colorado, and freefalling off of a beak-shaped mountain in North Carolina. You'll learn lessons about survival, friendship, leadership, travel, perseverance, and so much more! These are lessons that the Lord spoke to my soul, and I know they will help you grow in wisdom and maturity as you think through how they apply to your life. Ask God to speak to you in the pages of this book and to teach you the lessons he wants you to learn here.

Are you ready for an adventure?

1

THE CAVE DIVE

A s a boy growing up in frigid Minnesota, one of my dreams was to scuba dive in warm ocean waters. I dreamed of adventures like I saw on Jacques Cousteau's amazing underwater TV specials—just me, my breathing apparatus, and the big, beautiful sea. Jacques Cousteau didn't only walk on the wild side. He dove deep into it, air bubbles trailing behind him as he plunged into unexplored worlds below.

Bright-eyed, I watched his television shows teeming with fish of every kind and landscapes harsh and unexplored yet beautiful, colored like an underwater rainbow. I wanted to get right into the deep water and experience these incredible wonders for myself. In fact, I seriously considered becoming a marine biologist in high school. The underwater world called to me. So, I chose to go to New College on the Gulf Coast of Florida. Maybe if I got closer to the ocean, I could experience the wonder of scuba diving for myself.

Soon after arriving at New College, I made a friend. Like me, he was a first-year student. His name was Mitch Grandi, and he came from the greater San Francisco area. Mitch was smart as a whip and sarcastic in a funny and worldly way. My friend had to wear a leg brace due to a bout of polio he experienced when he was young.

Mitch dreamed of learning to scuba dive just like me. Together, we pursued our own Jacques Cousteau adventure. We became certified as scuba divers and took our first dives in the New College pool and, later, in the Gulf of Mexico.

In the Gulf, the water was warm but cloudy. The lack of clarity was a danger. Tiger sharks migrated along the coast of Florida, and Mitch and I believed if we saw one in the water, it would be the last thing we would ever see.

So, when we heard about a different kind of diving—cave diving—its apparent safety appealed to us. We knew that cave diving was very different from open-water diving. Cave diving is considered technical diving compared to the recreational diving we were trained to do, so cave diving requires an additional level of certification to ensure divers do not lose sight of the entrance and endanger their lives. We decided we didn't need the extra training.

This was our first in a cascade of almost-fatal errors.

A cascade is a small waterfall, typically one of several waterfalls that fall in stages down a steep rocky slope. A cascade of errors is a series of mistakes that cause you to fall into a very bad place, possibly even to your own death. Mitch and I ignored the fact that we didn't have a cave-diving certification, and as we continued on, many other errors would follow.

We heard of an underwater cave in northern Florida and set our sights there for our first cave dive. Thrilled for the adventure, we threw our scuba gear into an old, nearly broken-down car and drove to northern Florida.

The underwater cave looked like a small lake with a layer of lily pads on top. *Easy, like a swimming pool,* we thought. We put on our scuba gear—mask, fins, air tank, weight belt, buoyancy compensator and regulator—and slipped into the water.

Turning on our underwater flashlights, we swam deeper and began to look around. I was dumbstruck; I mean, absolutely flabbergasted. The water was so incredibly clear. I could see for over one hundred feet! The cave walls were made of limestone, and I could see every glorious stratum and cavity in the rock as they stretched into the depths.

Hanging there in the water, I reveled in being weightless. A small movement of my hands and fins was enough to propel me in any direction I chose. It was like flying in slow motion in a three-dimensional state. I could go up and down, over and around. I turned somersaults just because I could. It was incredible! I loved that feeling.

I saw Mitch to my left a few feet away and could tell he was experiencing the same wonder. Then I looked down. The depths entranced me. I wanted to go there. So I did. I left Mitch and headed straight down. This was the second error. I went alone to the bottom of the cave, which was about ninety feet below the surface.

There was a chimney hole at the bottom of the cave. It was just like a chimney in a house: a vertical passageway about four feet in diameter, room for only one diver. Despite my claustrophobia, I dove headfirst into that chimney. Third error. I flippered my way down through the four-foot-wide chimney. It seemed a long, long way down, but it was probably close to thirty feet.

If I had gotten stuck in the chimney, I don't know what I would have done because I was upside down in an underwater cave breathing from a tank of air. How do you back up in a situation like that?

At that depth, I was a little heavier than water. And so I fell in slow motion through the hole in the bottom of the chimney to the floor of a horizontal passageway. There was silt on the passage's floor. I started finning my way through this horizontal passage for another thirty feet. Fourth error.

My breathing began to be labored. I recognized the sign. It meant that I was running low on oxygen in my tank. Time to go back. I flipped around and was plunged immediately into a cloud of silt. The silt was all stirred up because I had fallen to the bottom and flippered along the cave floor. I faced a dense cloud of muddy, impossible darkness.

In shock, I waved my hand in front of my facemask to check visibility, but I could not even see my hand a couple inches in front of me. My flashlight was of no use either since the silt in the water completely diffused any light my flashlight tried to throw. Without light, I had no hope of finding my bearings so I could get out of there.

Fear gripped me. I was 120 feet deep in an underwater cave, running out of air, and I couldn't see three inches in front of my mask, let alone thirty feet back to a four-foot chimney hole.

I swam back to where I thought the chimney hole was. I knew there was no other way out. That chimney hole was my only path to life. I had to find that hole.

I put my hand up on the ceiling to search through the darkness for an escape. Solid rock. Desperately I felt along the roof. Still more rock. I couldn't find the hole. At that moment, I began to panic. I imagined myself searching and searching for that chimney only to gasp my last breath and die.

Death would have been the logical result of my cascade of errors. After all, I had made four huge mistakes that led me to this life-and-death moment.

Was I really going to drown in this underwater cave? That was horrifying! My breathing was becoming more and more labored. I was scared almost to death.

Just then, I saw a very dim glimmer in front of me, to the left. I immediately headed that direction. The light got brighter and the water got clearer as I got closer. It was Mitch's dive light. He was swimming down that chimney hole looking for me.

There are no words to describe how ecstatic and relieved I was to see him and his light. This was life, the light of life! Just moments before, I was absolutely certain I was going to die in that cave. Now, the powerful assurance of rescue washed over me. I was going to live!

Mitch was upside down in the chimney hole, facing me, and I pushed him backward through that thirty-foot chimney to the ninety-foot level of the cave bottom. Together, side by side, we swam for the surface.

When we got to the surface, I took the regulator out of my mouth and breathed in that sweet, sweet oxygen. I was alive!

When we reached the shore and took our gear off, I gave Mitch a big hug and thanked him from the bottom of my heart. This man had saved my life! I was running out of air, and if he hadn't come looking for me, I would have died in that cave.

He seemed a little surprised. "Just doing what we are trained to do—making sure my dive buddy was safe and sound."

Remember, a "cascade of errors" is a series of escalating errors, each one amplifying the effect of the previous one until they end in catastrophe.

In this cave dive, we didn't believe we needed advanced training to dive in caves. We believed that our open-water scuba certification was enough. Error.

Once we got in the water and began exploring, I went off by myself, leaving my buddy behind. Error.

Once I dropped to the floor of the horizontal passageway at 120 feet, I didn't recognize that I would stir up the silt so badly that I absolutely couldn't see. Error.

If we had been experienced cave divers, we would have attached a rope at the surface and taken it all the way down with us. That way, when my tank was running out of air and I turned around, I would have simply followed the rope back to the surface. No rope. Error.

This cascade of errors could have, and probably should have, cost me my life, but it didn't.

I lived because my buddy followed his training, and, at the risk of his own life, he found me and saved my life.

About a year later, I was reading the newspaper and found an article about the same cave that Mitch and I had dove into. Two young men, one from Minnesota like me, dove in that cave. They got lost, ran out of air, and drowned.

That caused me to wonder, *Why me? Why was I saved, and they weren't?* Though I was not a Christian then, I thought, *There must be some reason I am alive.* I just didn't know what it was at that point in my story.

What My Cave Dive Taught Me about Leadership

Now that I'm a leader of a global nonprofit organization, I look back at the cascade of errors in my and Mitch Grandi's cave dive, and I can see how young leaders back themselves into cascades of errors every day, some of which may be fatal to their organizations.

If you are a leader, you make choices every day. Your choices affect not only yourself and your job but also those you lead, your organization as a whole, and the people your organization serves. *So, how do leaders learn to make good decisions?* I believe the answer is to pivot. Often, bad decisions just happen. Continuing in that bad decision's path is what leads to demise. If you are a leader and you make a bad decision, recognize it, learn from it, and pivot.

In leadership, one bad decision does not need to move you down a road to destruction. Have you made a bad decision? Stop. Think. Realize you have made a bad decision. Everybody makes mistakes—all the time. Give yourself time to pray and think and make a good decision. Pray and ask God what to do. Don't make bad decision after bad decision after bad decision. That cascade of errors could send you and those you lead down a tunnel to catastrophe.

Proverbs 27:12 says, "The prudent see danger and take refuge, but the simple keep going and pay the penalty."

As a leader, when you start to recognize danger in your future, take refuge! You never have to keep going down the road to destruction.

What My Cave Dive Taught Me about Friendship

An even more powerful lesson from my cave-diving adventure is that good friends are incredibly valuable. I believe leaders need friends who can come alongside them with wisdom and grace and point them upward when leading is confusing, dark, and uncertain.

Ecclesiastes 4:12 says, "Though one may be overpowered, two can defend themselves. A cord of three strands is not quickly broken."

If you want to be the strongest, most resilient leader possible, you need friends. Friends can make the difference between surviving and running out of oxygen, between leading your organization well and finding yourself all alone and ready to give up the fight.

Whenever God calls you to a new adventure, ask him, "Who do you want me to bring along?" and "What do you want this person to do in this adventure?" You might be surprised at how God surrounds you with support, blesses you with relationships, and strengthens you as a leader in his kingdom!

What My Cave Dive Taught Me about Prayer and Planning

If you had told me when I was a little boy watching Jacques Cousteau on television that someday I would scuba dive and it would nearly kill me, I would probably open my blue eyes wide in both excitement and terror. If I had known beforehand what was going to happen, I wouldn't have made some of those foolish errors.

Despite my foolishness, this experience will stick with me for the rest of my life. It taught me to put adventure in the context of wisdom, faith, and methodical planning.

If you are anything like I was as a young person, it can be easy to associate wildness and adventure with spontaneity and risk. But, as I have grown as a man and a leader, I have chosen the opposite. Instead of plunging into the dangerous waters of unplanned adventures, I have become a kneeler. Before I go, I kneel before God in prayer. Before I make big decisions as a leader, I usually take a three-day prayer retreat to be sure I have heard from the Lord about my next steps. I try to never tell others my new ideas or initiatives without first laying them at the feet of the Lord who establishes our steps.

Proverbs 16:9 says, "In their hearts humans plan their course, but the LORD establishes their steps."

I pray first because on my own, without God's direction, big dreams can become big regrets. But, with God, dreams can flourish into far more than we could ask or imagine.

Ephesians 3:20–21 says, "Now to him who is able to do immeasurably more than all we ask or imagine, according to his power that is at work within us, to him be glory in the church and in Christ Jesus throughout all generations, for ever and ever! Amen."

When I pray about what's next and let him lead, my adventures become about God's glory! As he directs my plans and dreams, I get to jump in for a wild ride, watching his glory with astonishing wonder.

Even When I Was Far from God

As I look back on this experience, God was very present in my life. I just didn't see it. When I was far from God, when I was agnostic and had no regard for him, he saved my life and taught me about the horrible feeling of being lost. Even when I couldn't see him working, God was preventing my foolish cascade of errors from killing me because he had big plans for the years to come, when Paul Becker would surrender his life to everything God wanted to do with it.

The cave taught me that, even when we have no faith, God is faithful. Even when we are lost and cannot find a way out, God can provide an escape. Even when we are stuck in utter darkness, God can shine his saving light.

It wasn't until about seven years later, in a rented dorm room in Pittsburgh, that I would finally give my life to Christ. Just like my body was lost in the bottom of that cave in northern Florida, my soul was lost and hopeless in my sin, but God shined his light in my life and showed me the way to be saved, just as Mitch had done on that day in 1969.

In between the cave dive that almost ended my life and the weekend when I surrendered my life to Christ, I experienced some truly wild adventures, but nothing prepared me for the wonderful wildness of following Jesus Christ. Even though I did not believe in him, God was faithful in my life. In fact, my story isn't about my adventures at all. It's about a God who is faithful and adventurous. I just needed to receive his love and enjoy the ride of a lifetime!

So, wherever you find yourself on your spiritual journey, I invite you to pray this prayer: "Lord God, please show yourself to me." In every season, he is there. No matter how hard you try, you cannot push God out of your life. He made your life, and he desires to know you intimately. He desires to show you amazing and unforgettable things and to lead you out of darkness into a life of light, faith, and things more wild than you could ever dream.

LIFE LESSONS

- If you find yourself making a cascade of errors, stop, pray, and make a good decision about the way forward.
- Leaders need friends. Surround yourself with wise, godly friends. God can use them to protect you from harm and foolish decision making.
- Wild adventure doesn't mean poor planning. Before you leap, always kneel in prayer and ask God for wisdom first.
- Even when people do not believe in God, he is still actively working in their lives. His plans extend far beyond your current adventure.

WHAT ABOUT YOU?

1. Can you think of a time when you weren't really aware of or looking for God, but you can see his hand at work when you look back on that situation? What was it?

2. Have you experienced your own "cascade of errors"? What will you do in the future when you recognize an error or string of errors in your life?

3. Think of a time when a good friend really had your back. Have you thanked them?

4. God is faithful, even when we are not. God loves us even when we don't love him. Are you watching for God today? Will you ask him to reveal himself to you?

5. What is one area of your life that needs more prayer before you take the next step into the adventure?

2

THE WILDEST MENTOR
I EVER MET

"Life is either a daring adventure or nothing."

– HELEN KELLER, THE OPEN DOOR

Have you ever met someone who was so distinctly different from anyone you had ever met before that you were immediately captivated by them, and as you got to know them, they changed the way you saw the world forever?

When I was twelve years old, I sat down at a pine-wood table in an old classroom of Our Redeemer Lutheran Church in Maplewood, Minnesota, and met a man who changed my life forever. His name was Dr. Richard Reusch, and he was wilder than anyone I have ever met.

At the start of my confirmation training class, I had no idea how truly intrepid this new mentor of mine was. As a youth, I only knew Dr. Richard Reusch to be the associate pastor of our church. But as I got to know him, I discovered that there was not one season of his life that could be considered dull. And, because of his mentorship, my life has been way less dull than it would have been!

Reusch was born in Russia in 1891 to two German parents who brought him up as a strong Lutheran Christian. As a young adult, he served in the military under the czar of Russia, but they lost the Russian Revolution, and Dr. Reusch's family was exiled to Germany. There, he got ordained as a Lutheran pastor on Easter Sunday in 1917.

Then, in 1923, he took a wild leap and moved to Tanzania to serve as a Lutheran missionary for the next thirty-five years. Moving to Tanzania in the 1920s meant leaving modern civilization to engage with a people group and culture that was unlike any he'd experienced. There, he became a linguist, builder, storyteller, and honorary Maasai warrior.

In Tanzania, Dr. Reusch worked at the Teacher's Training School, where he taught his students the pillars of the Christian faith. He once told me that his students would walk two by two singing "Onward Christian Soldiers" as they moved around the school ground. I wonder if his service under the czar of Russia gave him a more robust picture of the wholehearted devotion of being a soldier for Christ. Certainly, the men and women shepherded by Dr. Reusch throughout the course of his life grasped a weightier understanding of the gospel as a result of his mentorship. I know I did!

He often said, "I love young people and helping them find Christ!" He did just that until the day he died.

He was a short man, about five feet, five inches tall, with wide shoulders. I remember the time he picked up a two-hundred-pound weight and lifted it over his head at the age of seventy-two. I was astounded. His vitality taught me that I should expect, as I grow older, to be strong because serving God is a lifelong adventure, not to be thwarted by an aging body.

Reusch spoke English with a captivating Russian accent. Some of the kids in confirmation class made fun of him. But I was told that he spoke ten languages and dialects of Swahili, which I respected immensely. I also respected him for his compelling stories. They transported me to another world.

His words took us to moments of great bravery, such as when he aggressively confronted domestic violence in Africa. His words took us on big game hunts, where he shot a lion that had been attacking the villages of his people around the base of Mount Kilimanjaro. His words took us across the deserts of Africa, into dangerous territory, and up the ascent of the highest mountain in Africa. His life was one adventure after another.

His refreshing perspective laid a foundation in my mind that following Christ was an all-in wonderfully adventurous endeavor. I wanted to go for it and not slow down when I was with Dr. Reusch. Great mentors have a way of opening your mind like Dr. Reusch did for me.

The Man for Whom They Named the Crater in Kilimanjaro

Dr. Reusch's adventurous spirit explored trails and topographies, wonders and worlds new and unknown, but his most repeated adventure was climbing Mount Kilimanjaro. This Wild Man for Jesus climbed Mount Kilimanjaro more than any other person who was not a native of Tanzania...ever. Google it! Dr. Reusch ascended Mount Kilimanjaro over sixty times.

Dr. Reusch often quoted Philippians 4:13 NLT: "I can do everything through Christ, who gives me strength."

He left quite an impression on the Tanzanian people. In fact, the crater in Mount Kilimanjaro is named for him, and the second highest elevation on the mountain, Elveda Point, is named for his American-born wife, a missionary nurse, Elveda Reusch.

Could I Climb Kilimanjaro?

In 2003, I reflected on Dr. Reusch's life and his impact on me as I stared at the north side of Kilimanjaro from my small gray camping chair in Kenya. This mountain towered above the clouds, reminding me of the courage of my late mentor and of the massiveness of the life I desired to live up to.

"Could I climb that mountain, Lord?" I asked as I looked at its height above the clouds.

I remembered that my mentor did, many times. Dr. Reusch's courage and audacity gave me confidence. He was an extraordinary man, and I wanted to live like he did in my own God-given way, in my own generation. So, in 2004, twenty-nine years after Dr. Reusch passed away, I took a walk on the wild side and climbed to the summit of Mount Kilimanjaro.

Living Like Dr. Reusch

There are tears in my eyes as I write about him. My life would be so much poorer without the rich teaching and example of Dr. Reusch, a true spiritual father to me. I couldn't orchestrate that meeting as a twelve-year-old boy. The Lord brought this spiritual guide for me as a gift, though I didn't know I needed it.

He was a living, breathing example of a man who endured hardship and found ways to thrive anywhere the Lord led him. That strengthened my faith and gave me more perseverance to move forward during hard times. He took the great risk to go to what is now Tanzania and serve the Lord, which encouraged me to take great faith steps throughout my own life. He told stories about the greatness of God in his life, and I have followed his lead.

He was a man of accomplishment in so many areas: his ministry, writing, language learning, even climbing Kilimanjaro. This taught me to be well rounded in getting things done in a variety of pursuits in life. Dr. Reusch was an anchor for my wild heart, tethering me to the God who has good and wild plans for my life.

Get Mentors and Learn All You Can from Them

Mentoring is the most powerful way of teaching and training another person. This is especially true in the Bible. Moses mentored Joshua. Elijah mentored Elisha. Barnabas mentored Paul. Paul mentored a team of people to take the Mediterranean world for Christ. If you don't have a Wild Man or Wild Woman of Jesus to be your mentor, pray and ask God for the right mentor to come into your life. Then ask that mentor to meet with you.

Some mentors will come into your life for short seasons. Others will be around for quite a while. Some mentorships are more formal, and others are casual friendships. Whomever God leads into your life, in whatever season, open your eyes, ears, and heart to glean wisdom from them. Their example may plant itself deep into your soul and shape the way you live for decades to come.

One day, as a teenager, I went to my dentist, another member of our church. He said to me, "Dr. Reusch was in my office recently. He told me you were going to be a pastor." I was shocked. It had never occurred to me to become a pastor. I didn't want to be a pastor. But I remembered that prediction in my heart long into my future.

Dr. Reusch's personal, powerful relationship with God, the teaching and mentoring that this Mighty Man of God sowed into my life, and his unforgettable stories poured a foundation in my soul of what it could be like to follow an unimaginably huge, amazingly powerful, and wildly adventurous God. Through Dr. Reusch and the memories I held of him, the God of the universe poured his love into my life even before I truly recognized him.

Good spiritual mentors have a powerful and subtle way of steering your soul away from sin and toward adventure with the God who loves you. Though these relationships may seem uneventful, never underestimate their power in your life.

Ask them questions about how they do things and what God is doing in their lives. Share your experiences and ask for their insight. My guess is that it will be the everyday, normal interactions with your mentor that open the door for God to speak truth into your heart.

Your Life Doesn't Have to Be Secure

One of the deepest truths God spoke into my heart through Dr. Reusch was that my life doesn't have to be predictable, planned out, and secure.

Unlike my father and grandfather before me, I decided not to become an accountant. Instead, I pursued the financially unpredictable career of fulltime ministry. Dr. Reusch taught me that my life doesn't have to be confined to the bounds of what I think is normal. I live by faith, and what an adventure it has been so far! God has allowed me to visit 102 countries, meeting extraordinary people of God all around the world, and seeing God plant nearly a million churches through Dynamic Church Planting International (DCPI).

In 2004, I even had the marvelous delight of being named an honorary Maasai warrior, like my most respected mentor. Like Dr. Reusch's, my shoes are covered with the scuffs of global travels, scrapes from the persistent pursuit of lost people, and the dust of Mount Kilimanjaro. Because of Dr. Reusch's example in my life, God has opened the world to me, and I have seen beauty and experienced miracles my mind could never have imagined!

Now that I am a grandfather, looking toward the next generation and the generation after that, I am moved to recognize that God steers our lives like rudders, gently turning us this way and that, bringing into our lives mentors to direct our steps, shape our paradigm, and empower us to build the character and fortitude of heart that God will use in our lives and ministries down the road.

You don't have to be scared of what God might call you to do. He loves you! He has good plans for you! He will provide for you, and, if you trust him, he will lead you on adventures you never dreamed of! Yes, God can use your gifts and talents to expand his kingdom around the world, but I am convinced that *you* will receive the biggest blessings of all, as he allows your eyes to behold and your soul to take in the beauty and majesty of serving a God who reigns over this whole earth—an earth that he made to be both wild and wonderful because he is good.

LIFE LESSONS

- Get a mentor and observe his/her life closely. God may use that person to speak truth that will stick with you for your lifetime.

- Your life doesn't have to be secure in a worldly way because you serve a stable and powerful God who can lead you on adventures you never dreamed of and provide for everything as you walk by faith.

WHAT ABOUT YOU?

1. Have you ever had a mentor? If so, who was it, and what did he or she teach you?

2. When you envision your future, what appeals to you about having a stable career and safe life? What appeals to you about adventuring for God?

3. What is the next wild adventure you believe God is calling you to step into?

4. Are you scared of living a wild life for God? Write down some of your fears and hesitations, then pray for God to give you eyes to see your future in light of his goodness.

5. Living a wild life for God will look different for everyone, so take some time to pray for God to reveal to you *your* unique gifts, talents, and passions and to show you the big and small ways you could use the gifts he's given you.

6. Do you currently have a mentor? If not, whom do you need to talk to about meeting with you?

7. Who would be blessed to have you as a mentor? Be a mentor who is deeply in love with Jesus and help speak truth into their lives.

3

SAILING ALONE AROUND AN ISLAND

> *"Twenty years from now you will be more disappointed by the things you didn't do than by the ones you did. So, throw off the bowlines, sail away from the safe harbor, catch the trade winds in your sails. Explore. Dream. Discover."*
>
> **–H. JACKSON BROWN**

Perseverance...oh, perseverance. It's probably one of the most important lessons of the Christian life, but it's never comfortable to build perseverance. For me, my first major lesson in perseverance came on a solo sailing adventure I had in college.

I selected a nontraditional route when I chose to attend New College in Sarasota, Florida. Instead of a college education focused on bookwork and class time, mine was about traveling and interacting with people and places far away, which culminated in three large independent study projects and a senior project thesis. New College was a great place for self-directed people, and it was a perfect fit for me. I loved adventure, and I wanted to experience it all. What I didn't foresee was that some of these independent study projects would be absolutely miserable, life-threatening, and downright exhausting! But I also didn't foresee how these experiences would shape my life forever.

One of the projects I chose was to write a series of short stories about a Caribbean island. To get there, I hitchhiked to the Miami, Florida, airport, where I foolishly ran across a runway to get to a small airplane company, where I thought I could air-hitchhike to the Bahamas. A truck intercepted me on the runway, and I got into big trouble. I never did air-hitchhike to the Bahamas. Eventually, I took a one-way flight to the US Virgin Islands, where I would stay for the next month. Before I got off the airplane, I had a job offer to help one of the travelers with his grocery delivery business. After we arrived, I made the move to the island of St. John, preparing sailboats for the windy Christmas season.

I spent my project time writing stories, exploring Cruz Bay, and snorkeling. Once, I broke my eardrum diving on an old shipwreck in Coral Bay. This caused bleeding from my ear for a week or two, but the bleeding eventually stopped and my hearing improved.

As my time on the island of St. John was ending, I still held on to one dream: to circumnavigate St. John by myself, which meant to sail around the entire island. Alone.

Based on my maps and conversations with the locals, this trip looked to be about sixty miles. Determined to accomplish my mission, I rented a Sunfish sailboat to carry me around St. John. *How hard could it be, right?*

My Lone Voyage

The Sunfish is a single-hull sailboat that is about fourteen feet long and four feet wide. Though it was small, it was all I could afford to rent as a college student. As soon as I got the boat into the water, I slipped the daggerboard through the hull and vertically down into the water just behind the mast for stability. I strapped my pack over the top of the daggerboard. Then I set sail out of Cruz Bay on the western end of the island and tacked north and east toward Jost Van Dyke, an island in the British Virgins.

The water was warm. I reached my hand down and ran my fingers through the salty waves. Mist splashed my face, making me feel alive! The sun was hot. The breeze was light. I was exultant as I began to fulfill my sailing dream.

About halfway to Jost Van Dyke, I saw a *huge* manta ray leap out of the water just a few yards to the left (the port) side of my little sailboat. Then I heard the mighty crash of the creature as it hit the water. Astonishment and fear filled me. The largest mantas are almost three thousand pounds with a width of eighteen to twenty-two feet. I knew immediately and terrifyingly that this manta was *much bigger* than I and my Sunfish sailboat.

I suddenly felt like a small person on a small boat in the middle of a huge ocean. Though I could see land almost my entire time, I was aware of how small I was. What else swam beneath me in this water that was as big as a semitruck?

Sailing on, I beached my boat on the small island of Jost Van Dyke, where a famous little bar called Foxy's Bar still sits on the sand to this day. I headed over to Foxy's Bar (named after its owner) and lunched on a Caribbean lobster right on the beach. Delicious! There, I asked about uninhabited islands on which to spend the night. There were two choices: Mosquito Key and Sandy Key. Which one would you choose?

For obvious reasons, I chose Sandy Key. Would anyone willingly select an island called Mosquito Key? I sailed over, unloaded my gear, and set up my tent. Thus began the worst night of my life.

I got in my tent and zipped the screen door shut to keep out the mosquitoes. Yes, Sandy Key did indeed have mosquitoes. Unfortunately, the island was also infested with sandflies. In Florida, we called them "no-see-ums" because they are so miniscule they are very hard to see. They flew through my tent screen door easily and zeroed in on any exposed flesh they could find. Ouch! Ouch! I was bitten again and again for the next two hours of my life.

My only defense seemed to be to crawl into my sleeping bag and zip myself up. But it was ninety degrees Fahrenheit and humid outside and inside. I felt like I was bathing in my own sweat. Yuck! My head began to whirl amidst my own heat, misery, and frustration. No wonder this island was uninhabited. Nobody was stupid enough to live here or sleep here even for one night.

The sandflies continued to bite me. Their bite is painful and itches more than a mosquito's. No sleep could be found here. In the middle of the night, I realized that my only salvation from sandflies was the wind. I needed a breeze to blow the sandflies away, so I got out of the tent, braved the "no-see-ums" and the mosquitoes, and went searching for someplace on the island that had a breeze. Heading down the hill from where I had been "resting," I desperately searched for wind. I found a light breeze down on the beach.

It was truly beautiful, being alone on a deserted island. I could see tons of stars because there was no ground light. I adored the sound of the waves crashing nearby. I took delight in these small things and tried to forget the misery of my past few hours.

The sweet sea breeze offered me relief and a new wave of motivation. I moved my gear to that spot, set up my tent, and settled in for the rest of the night. Finally, the sweetness of sleep swept over me. Then, suddenly, though I have no concept of how long I slept, something else swept over me and my tent—a wave.

Surprise! Then another wave crashed, and another hit me. Everything was sloshing around inside my tent, including me. My tent felt more like an overflowing bathtub than a tent. I got out of my water-soaked bag and found my way out of the tent, thankfully. There was nothing to do but drag all my water-logged gear higher up the shore.

What had happened to me? How did I miscalculate my location enough to get hit by a series of waves?

Then I figured it out: I had camped below the high-tide mark. The tide had come up in the night. The waves that had previously been crashing out to sea were breaking on me.

Disgusted! That's how I felt. This was just wrong. It was nasty, and it was my fault. I felt frustrated and ashamed. What a rookie mistake!

Does this sound like an island paradise to you?

The rest of the night I spent sitting on a log on the beach looking toward the east and waiting for the dawn. Have I mentioned perseverance is uncomfortable? Boy, was I frustrated! Finally, after what seemed like an eternity of misery, the dawn peered over the watery horizon. "Time to get off this miserable island," I consoled myself.

I wanted to quit. After stowing my wet gear on the Sunfish, I could see myself heading back to Cruz Bay. How nice that would be! In front of me lay the comfortable opportunity of getting back to Cruz Bay, taking a refreshing shower, and sleeping in an air-conditioned room. But also before me stood my audacious dream of sailing the entire sixty miles around St. John. Should I go west toward comfort or east toward the unknown?

When the time came, I pushed off and tacked to the east to continue my circumnavigation of the island. *Surely the worst is behind me*, I assured myself.

I sailed south and then east into the Sir Francis Drake Channel between St. John and Tortola. Out of nowhere, the wind died. I was becalmed. That's what sailors call it when there is no wind. No wind means no sailing. Just a hint of wind was blowing very lightly into my face. When this happens, the best solution is to maneuver the boat back and forth, right and left, to pick up some wind in the sails. I tried tacking back and forth in my little sailboat for most of the morning and into the early afternoon, but I barely moved at all. It didn't seem like I was making any headway in my attempt to sail around the island of St. John.

As a self-proclaimed sailing rookie, I wondered what the sailors on the great wooden ships of centuries past did when they were becalmed for days and weeks at a time. I clenched my fists as I confronted layer upon layer of frustration. No wind was only my latest in a series of self-doubts that beckoned me to turn this Sunfish back around and head toward the comforts of civilization.

This sailing trip was not going the way I wanted it to go. The convenience of turning west back to Cruz Bay called to me. It would mean the end of this ridiculous trip, but it would also mean defeat and the end of this dream. I chose to stay my course.

By midafternoon, the wind picked up a little. I finally made a little headway. The boat crossed the east end of St. John and beyond to Norman Island. Hope arose within me, and I thought, *This might be just a little bit fun!*

Norman Island is famous for being one of the islands that inspired Robert Louis Stevenson to write his famous tale *Treasure Island*. Indeed, there is a history of pirate treasure being buried and recovered on Norman Island, but I didn't find any. I pulled my boat to shore and did a little snorkeling, including trying to pull a lobster out of its hole in the coral. After I pulled and pulled on the antennae of this large red critter, its determination outlasted mine, and I gave up. It had a stronger will to live than I had to eat it.

From there, I pushed out to sea again and sailed to the "west-northwest." The wind picked up. My little boat was sailing perfectly with the wind. I have noticed that, in most transformative experiences of life, there's a point of severe discomfort that causes you to consider giving up before the hope of victory starts to come within grasp. That's when the joy sets in! The fun of this experience splashed onto my face with each ocean mist as I cruised my way into Coral Bay of St. John.

A few weeks before, I had made friends with a family who owned a vacation home on Coral Bay. When I pulled my sailboat into Coral Bay, I asked the caretaker of the home, and he let me spend the night there. Sweet rest swept over my tired body.

The next morning, I thanked the caretaker and headed south. I rounded Ram Head and headed west. The wind was strong and steady, and, again, I grinned at the splendor of surging ahead full speed through the waves. My little sailboat was "heeling over"! This is the beautiful thing that happens when a sailboat leans to the side in the water as it is being driven by the wind. I reveled in the victory of this smooth, glorious sailing experience that I had only dreamed about. What a thrill! There's nothing else like it. Your sails fill and you take off like a shot.

Mile after mile, I hydroplaned along the south coast of St. John. I was exhilarated! *This* was the experience I had dreamed about.

Finally, I sailed beyond St. John, farther than I had originally intended on going, to a coral reef I had heard about, and found myself closely approaching. This was Great St. James Island, just off the west coast of St. Thomas. I looked down into the crystal blue water and realized I was sailing over a coral reef. It. Was. Right. There. Just below me! It seemed like it was just a few inches under, and my daggerboard was sticking three feet into the water.

Was I going to crash into the reef? If my daggerboard struck coral, it would flip my boat. Alarmed, I scrambled to loosen my pack and pull my daggerboard into the cockpit. Safely passing the coral reef, I sighed in relief and set my eyes toward the end of my journey—Cruz Bay.

Pride Goes before a Fall

It was a good sail as I entered the harbor. I could even see a few of my friends on the dock looking my way and waving. Sweet victory! I was looking good. The sailboat was heeling over a bit. With a smug smile on my face, I was thinking, *I bet my friends think I'm cool!*

Just then, the fifty-foot ferryboat from St. Thomas motored by me with a surprisingly big wake. When the wake hit my little boat, my pack shifted down since I hadn't tied it off. My daggerboard was not in the water to stabilize the boat, and I flipped.

When I got the Sunfish righted, I was hit by another wake and flipped again. Finally, I got it together and made it to the dock, a little humiliated but happy to have fulfilled my dream of sailing all around the island.

Laughing at me, one of my friends said, "Must have been a tough trip with all that flipping."

I thought about saying, "The only two times I flipped were right here, right now," but I didn't think they would believe me.

Humiliated and wet, I had seized the victory. I had overcome mosquitoes, sandflies, waves flooding my tent, a sleepless night, becalming, coral reefs, and large wakes. Though I had made rookie mistakes, I arrived back in one piece. I felt overwhelmed, relieved, and proud.

The Song of Perseverance

Perseverance was the song I had learned to sing. If I hadn't persevered beyond the worst night of my life, if I hadn't kept sailing when I was becalmed, and if I hadn't kept my course to circle the island, then I would have missed that glorious sail on the last day. More importantly, I would have given up on my dream to circumnavigate St. John.

Here is a great quote from Barbara Stewart, the director of Endeavor Management:

> *"Determination is focus on the purpose. Persistence is the continuation of action around that purpose. Both are required for success. Determination brings the clarity of 'I have decided,' while persistence describes the action necessary and then helps you carry it forward."*[1]

---

1   Barbara Stewart, "What Is the Difference between Determination and Persistence?" Endeavor, https://www.acceluspartners.com/what-is-the-difference-between-determination-and-persistence/.

Throughout my life of ministry and missions, I have needed perseverance more times than I can count. Ministry is hard. People's lives are messy. Finances are scarce. Politics can interrupt the work God is doing. People can say harsh things that cut deep. Life can get exhausting. When we're called to serve God, we set our eyes on him who refreshes our souls and gives us strength to persevere.

After all, Jesus endured the cross, and now he is seated at the right hand of the throne of God (Hebrews 12:2). And we have a great cloud of witnesses both on earth and in heaven cheering us on to persevere in following Christ and throwing off sin until our last breath (Hebrews 12:1).

In our world of quick fixes and shortcuts, it can require true character and strength from God to persevere. Our Christian life is dependent upon our perseverance. As we follow Jesus, we set our eyes on our destination, and we continue sailing toward him. We may experience setbacks, adversity, self-doubt, pain, loss, embarrassment, and more, but we have the assurance that he is always with us and leading us toward our ultimate destination, our heavenly home.

Though at the time of this sailing trip I considered myself agnostic, I can see now that God was steering my heart as I endured those waves back in 1970. In the hardest moments of the trip, I was wondering, questioning what I was doing and if I had what it took to fulfill my mission. Then, as victory came into view, pride set in. My pride came before a fall, and my boat flipped twice right in front of my friends. Then I arrived safely on shore and experienced the joy of perseverance.

Living the Christian life can be like that. The beginning is invigorating and exciting. Then it can get hard, uncomfortable, and trying, almost as if we're beckoned to turn back. But, in the midst of the trial and the pain, there's grace. God's presence sustains us like a brand-new sunrise and a way out of the darkness. Then there's victory and joy. And when pride comes, we get humbled. But ultimately it is God's faithfulness with us through the whole journey that enables us to arrive at home, where Jesus himself will say, "Well done, my good and faithful servant."

So, if you are tempted to turn back from ministry or your walk with Jesus at any point, remember these words, "Let us not become weary in doing good, for at the proper time we will reap a harvest if we do not give up" (Galatians 6:9).

Day by day, as you persevere in following Christ and serving however he calls you to serve, you are doing the work of planting seeds. He is the One who grows them, and he is the One who brings the harvest.

In the middle of the hard parts, the harvest is on its way.

In the middle of the darkness and discomfort, the harvest is on its way.

In the middle of the loneliness and frustration, the harvest is on its way.

In the middle of the doubt and insecurity, the harvest is on its way.

When you fall down from pride and are humbled, the harvest is on its way.

Don't give up, my dear friend. The harvest is on its way, and someday, you're going to arrive on that shore to see Jesus face to face. Then all the pain will fade away, and he will wipe every tear from your eye, and you'll be home.

Please don't give up.

LIFE LESSON

- When life gets hard, it's tempting to turn toward comfort and convenience instead of persevering, but we will reap the harvest if we don't give up.

WHAT ABOUT YOU?

1. Think of a situation in your life when you really wanted to give up, but instead you persevered. How did that feel?

2. Memorize Galatians 6:9: "Let us not become weary in doing good, for at the proper time we will reap a harvest if we do not give up," and recite it to yourself whenever you are tempted to give up.

3. And/or memorize Hebrews 12:1–3: "Therefore, since we are surrounded by such a great cloud of witnesses, let us throw off everything that hinders and the sin that so easily entangles. And let us run with perseverance the race marked out for us, fixing our eyes on Jesus, the pioneer and perfecter of faith. For the joy set before him he endured the cross, scorning its shame, and sat down at the right hand of the throne of God. Consider him who endured such opposition from sinners, so that you will not grow weary and lose heart." Recite it to yourself whenever you are tempted to give up.

4. What is one area of your life where you currently have to persevere? How does it feel to be in the middle of the

battle? What do you think it's going to feel like when the battle is over and you've reaped the harvest?

5. Who or what can motivate you to persevere?

4

KIBBUTZING
AROUND ISRAEL

*"You will never be completely at home again,
because part of your heart always will be elsewhere.
That is the price you pay for the richness of loving
and knowing people in more than one place."*

–MIRIAM ADENEY

When I was in high school, I dreamed of living on a kibbutz in Israel as a young adult. The book *The Source*, written by James Michener, opened my mind to a fascinating world of communal living unlike anything I'd seen in the suburbs of the United States. This historical fiction tale, set in the Holy Land, spans many centuries from prehistory through the 1948 War for Independence and beyond. As I pored over the pages of this epic saga, I dreamed of going to Israel for myself to live on a kibbutz, to interact firsthand with people who thought so differently about the world, and to have their way of life change me.

Kibbutz is a Hebrew word meaning "gathering" or "clustering." It is a collective community in Israel where people live together, provided for by the income generated from their specific trade. The number of kibbutzim—the plural word for kibbutz—grew rapidly between 1910 and 1948 all over Palestine. Most kibbutzim were set up by agricultural workers, but later, other trades began forming kibbutzim as well. When the Arab–Israeli War came in 1948, these kibbutzim became military strongholds for the Jews. It is very unlikely that the Jews would have won the war without this network of communal farms.

Was it really true that people could live like this and thrive as a society? Specifically, what were they like? The idea of communal living, remnants of wartime bravery, and shared reciprocity among residents sounded so unique and vibrant that I had to see it for myself. In college, I kept my eyes open for opportunities to jump into a kibbutz adventure. My university, New College in Florida, encouraged students to design independent study projects, and I immediately knew one of my projects would be a six-month study of the kibbutz high school educational system in Israel. I wanted to know how kibbutz living affected these people's worldviews and their lives and work, especially the high school students.

It was 1971, and I had just turned twenty. The program began in January 1972, so I celebrated Christmas with my family in St. Paul, Minnesota, before flying to Israel and becoming a volunteer worker on a kibbutz. I didn't know to which kibbutz I would be assigned, only that I couldn't wait to start the adventure! I had a layover in New York City, where I boarded my El Al flight to Tel Aviv. The flight was uneventful, except that I met two new friends—David and Tony—who were about my age and also going to volunteer on a kibbutz. When we arrived at the Kibbutz Volunteers Program Center in Tel Aviv, they weren't ready for us and asked us to come back in a couple of days.

Perfect, I thought. *This is my opportunity to explore the Old City of Jerusalem. What a wonder!*

But first, we needed food. We sat down for a meal of "mystery meat" in an Arab restaurant hidden in the Old City. This is where I learned my rule number one for international travel: don't eat mystery meat! Ever. I added this to my Mental Notes for Adventurers that would later include: Don't eat roadkill monitor lizards in Indonesia. Don't eat goat liver cooked on an open fire in northwest Kenya. Just drink bottled water (and pray that someone hasn't just poured tap water into it and put the cap back on). Just stay in good hotels that have good, healthy food for you to eat. Oh, I could go on and on, but these are all stories for my later two books. As you can see, I sometimes learn things the hard way. That night in Jerusalem was one of those hard ways.

That meal tasted fine, but as we were on our way back to Tel Aviv for placement on a kibbutz, I started to feel sick. They placed all three of us on Kibbutz Usha, a farming community, which meant a trip north along the coast until we came to Haifa. Every bump and turn made my stomach feel like it was sloshing from side to side. From there, we traveled east a few miles to Kiryat Ata. Kibbutz Usha was just outside of town.

When we arrived, waves of nausea overwhelmed my "hellos" and caused the people to send me straight to bed. I was deathly ill. Awful liquids were leaving both ends of my body. I was in real pain and felt like I was going to die. To this day, I don't think I have ever been that sick. Through it all, the people on the kibbutz were very kind to me. Yet they wondered whether they should send me home, and I begged to stay. They relented, watching to see what would happen to me. In two days, I was over the worst of it and starting to feel better.

Emerging from my dorm room at last, I got to know a man named Moishe (Moses). Moishe was an old man from the kibbutz who interviewed David, Tony, and me. He then led us out before the gathering of the kibbutzniks—the people who lived on the kibbutz—to introduce us.

Moishe said, "This is David. He is a Jew. This is Tony. He is a Christian. And this is Paul. He is a nothing."

I had told him that I was an agnostic, someone who had no knowledge of God. It was funny, and we all laughed when Moishe called me a "nothing." In fact, every time I think back to this moment, I laugh out loud. It was a moment in time when someone said something that was both true and funny. I knew I was going to enjoy learning from these people for the next six months.

My Work on the Kibbutz

One of my first jobs on Kibbutz Usha was to "schlep" bananas. This is a Yiddish word based on German that means to haul or carry something heavy or awkward. The banana field was on top of a gentle hill. The field was watered so heavily that there were lanes of mud between the bananas. My job was to follow a "cutter," whose job was to go to a stem of green bananas weighing sixty-five to one hundred pounds and cut it down for me. Here's how I managed to move such an awkward and slightly fragile load: As the cutter and I approached the banana tree, I leaned into the banana stem with my shoulder at about the midpoint of the banana cluster. The cutter then severed the stem, and I carried the load over my right shoulder and slogged through the mud to bring the banana stem to the wagon. This was hard and somewhat awkward, but I liked it. I spent my mornings hard at work schlepping bananas.

One of my favorite activities in the afternoons was to sit down with older kibbutzniks who had been in the Holy Land since the 1930s and

1940s. They would tell their stories of leaving the ghettos of Europe and arriving in Palestine, training for battle, gathering at the kibbutz, working to plant their fields, and defending their home from the Arabs in the 1948 war. These people were as tough as nails!

After about a month of getting settled and enjoying the rhythm of good, hard work, I took a little time off and traveled north along the coast to Acre. Acre is a gorgeous and ancient walled city that towers above the Mediterranean Sea, surrounded on three sides by water. While in Acre, some Arabic schoolchildren wanted me to play kickball with them. We had a great time, until I kicked the ball especially hard and it sailed over the wall into the sea thirty-five feet below. The kids demanded money because I had lost their ball. Angry adults started to join the group. I thought it was wise to pay them. Then, as soon as I did, one of the boys threw his rope ladder over the wall and went down to collect the ball. If this had been an outsmarting match, the Arab kids would have earned a point and I, Paul, would have zero. But I laughed at this memorable and strangely delightful experience.

Back at the kibbutz, I worked for another two months before I left Kibbutz Usha to complete my study of the high school educational system on Kibbutz Revadim, which was farther south, about halfway between Ashkelon and Jerusalem. This kibbutz was razed to the ground in the war of 1948 with the Arabs. Later that year, after the Jews won their independence, this kibbutz was re-established. I loved being in a place with so many layers of history! And yet, despite all the glorious religious history, I still had no inclination to consider a relationship with God. I did, however, learn a whole new way of life that shaped my perspective on hard work and community relationships forever.

Catching Turkeys

On Kibbutz Revadim, my job was to catch turkeys and pick oranges. When I was assigned to the groves, I filled up large cubic bins measuring four feet across with the oranges I picked. If I could get three bins filled in a morning, I completed my work. I loved to eat delicious Jaffa oranges in the grove. Sometimes, I had dreams at night of the labor I did all day—picking the oranges, putting them in the bag tied around my waist, and placing them in the bin. It was difficult but invigorating work.

On a kibbutz, hard work is highly valued. Both the kibbutzniks and the volunteers were judged by how hard they worked. Hard workers were affirmed, often verbally. Those who shirked their responsibilities were criticized and shunned. Thankfully, I was considered a hard worker. This is where it was reinforced to me that "people you respect, respect hard work." This principle has carried me throughout my career. Hard work earns you admiration, relationships, and opportunities.

My hard work of catching turkeys was actually considered a prestigious job on the kibbutz. And the more I did it, the more skilled I became. Around eleven at night, we would gather at the turkey pens. The butchers, who were also rabbis to ensure that the turkeys would be kosher, would arrive in their truck with the empty turkey cages. At this point in the night, the turkeys were in a state of somnolence, or near-sleep. They would still be walking about, but they were much easier to catch than in the daytime. It took some practice, but as I mastered turkey catching, I got into a groove.

I would go through the pen, grab both legs of a turkey, lift it so that the turkey was hanging upside down, and place it in my left hand. Then I would do it again and place the feet of the second turkey in my left hand. Then, if I could, I would catch one more turkey with my right hand and head to the cages with all three birds. After we turkey catchers caught our quota for the day, the rabbi-butchers would drive to Jerusalem to butcher the turkeys in a kosher way and sell them in the market to earn income for the kibbutz. The turkey workers, like me, would have a massive meal of fruits, vegetables, and the less good turkey at two in the morning. We enjoyed what was produced on the kibbutz, but I was always a little concerned about eating bad turkey meat, especially after my experience in Jerusalem a few months earlier.

As a turkey worker, another responsibility I had was feeding the turkeys. One day, I discovered just how ornery a turkey can be. As I walked through a pen of fully awake birds, they peeled off to both sides in front of me and come around behind. Suddenly, one came up from behind and pecked at my leg. I kicked it. As soon as I did, the other turkeys charged at me, and soon I was kicking like a Russian hopak dancer to avoid being overwhelmed by hundreds of turkeys pecking at me.

An experienced turkey worker came to my rescue. When he immigrated to Israel, like others, he could choose his own Hebrew name. He chose Yom Tov, which means "Good Day" in Hebrew. Good Day said to me, "No, Paul, that is the wrong way. Turkeys are not very bright and they don't look up." Yom Tov found the first offending turkey, grabbed it by its throat, and tossed it over a ten-foot wire into another pen. Ouch! This did calm all the other turkeys and me, too.

A Communal Way of Life

Aside from learning the fundamentals of hard work and turkey catching, I did spend time analyzing the high school system of the kibbutz. At the time, the education system in the kibbutz was very communal. From the time these children were babies, they lived with one another and not with their parents. The children lived in their own houses overseen by "metapelets," or women who cared for babies and children. Their parents would visit them and sometimes bring them to their homes during the afternoons or on weekends. Each child received twelve years of education. There were no tests and no grades, and teaching was done in a multidisciplinary manner with lots of physical work on the kibbutz. As a result, the *group* was more highly prized than the *individual*. I concluded that these young people would do well in jobs and organizations that emphasized the group over the individual, like the armed services or corporations.

This was in contrast to me at that point in my development. I was more interested in finding projects that reflected my dreams and completing them, taking initiative to get what I wanted out of life. This striking difference started to shift my thinking.

In fact, many of their ways of life shifted my thinking. To this day, I have learned to embrace cultural differences as opportunities to learn and to build bridges with people in other cultures so that I can share the Good News about Jesus with them. I have found that, by humbling myself, I can embrace culture shock and differences as learning opportunities, and God can use these to shape me and to call people to himself.

Since the 1970s, the kibbutzim movement has undergone remarkable changes in the education system. The kibbutzniks wanted their children to live at home and not in the children's house, so communal sleeping arrangements came to an end. Examinations and standardization of teaching methods arrived. Younger generations began to leave kibbutz life for bigger cities, and the kibbutzim shifted to private ownership. Kibbutz life shifted from collectivism to individualism, much like the rest of modern society.

Festival Celebrations

While on Kibbutz Revadim, I experienced two festivals right out of the Bible. The first was Purim, which is a celebration of the story of Esther and the salvation of the Jewish people. The second was Pesach or Passover, which is when Moses led the Jews out of Egypt.

I was an agnostic, someone with no knowledge of God, and yet the celebration of Passover on the kibbutz surprised me because of how nonreligious it was. In the story of the first Passover, when the Jews reached the shore of the Red Sea and the Red Sea was parted, the people of Israel walked across. Then the soldiers of Egypt chased the Jews across the Red Sea, and the sea swallowed the soldiers up. There was absolutely no mention of God.

"Who parted the Red Sea?" I wondered out loud with some of my kibbutz friends. There was no answer.

I was on an atheistic kibbutz and we were celebrating these festivals as important cultural events, not religious and historical events. Though I was in the "Holy Land," this whole experience did not make me consider adopting a faith.

Seeing Israel

From the kibbutz, my friends and I dove into many adventures in Israel. We snorkeled in the Red Sea and saw huge brain coral and sea snakes. We climbed Masada by the narrow, winding Snake Path at night. Masada, which means "fortress," is a mountain plateau overlooking the Dead Sea. This was the last refuge of the Jews in the First Jewish–Roman War. The siege by the Romans in AD 73 and 74 ended in the mass suicide of 960 Jews according to Josephus. This is why during the wars that the Israelis have fought, they cry, "Remember Masada!"

We also visited Jerusalem and walked where Jesus walked: up the Via Dolorosa, the path that he took after his sentencing on the way to his crucifixion, to Gethsemane, where Jesus prayed the night before he was turned over to the Romans to be crucified. We went into the Church of the Holy Sepulchre, which is one of the sites where they believe Jesus may have died on the cross. I knew about these places because of my Lutheran confirmation, but I didn't know Jesus. Though faith came later, I was enamored by the rich history and tradition in Israel. Though I had spent my teenage years dreaming of the things I could see and experience in Israel, nothing quite prepared me for the way Israel would change me.

Adventure Changes You

Perhaps the reason I have become a lifelong adventurer is that I have seen how adventure changes you. In my travels as a college student, and even as a young adult, I saw things and experienced cultures that forever informed the way I think and relate to the world around me. Going somewhere far away and being with people who are very different from you is a phenomenal learning experience. When you uncover how other people live and love and serve and eat and die, it brings into question the assumptions you have made about your own world, causing you to be intentional about the way you live your life.

Maybe this is why I am so passionate about writing books and helping young adult Christians adventure. When you go, you see, and what you see changes you. When you go beyond yourself and discover a new place and people—perhaps by joining an international missions trip, or traveling with a group of people—you gain an appreciation for other cultures and the ways they do things that are very different from your home culture.

You don't need to be afraid of differences. Sitting down for a meal with someone different than you, both at home and abroad, can be surprisingly comfortable, interesting, and eye-opening. You may become enamored by the beauty of their culture, and your heart may grow as you realize that God loves them just as much as he loves you.

LIFE LESSONS

- Be very careful about what you eat and drink during your travels. You risk ruining a trip or worse. Don't eat mystery meat!
- Learn from people who are very different from you. This develops a love and appreciation for people from different cultures. Jesus loves each one of them as much as he loves you.
- Working hard earns you admiration, relationships, and opportunities.
- Adventure changes you. When you uncover how other people live and love and serve and eat and die, it brings into question the assumptions you have made about your own world, causing you to be intentional about the way you live your life.

WHAT ABOUT YOU?

1. What places or people around the world fascinate you enough that you would like to visit?
2. What book or show or Internet search or person planted this fascination in you?
3. What are some experiences that you hope to have in this new place and among these people?
4. How will you communicate your love for Jesus with these new people?
5. Do you have any rules for international travel? What are they? (Hint: one of mine is *no* mystery meat.)

5

YOU CAN DO THIS!

"To strive, to seek, to find, and not to yield."
–ALFRED, LORD TENNYSON, "ULYSSES"

A s I approached the edge of the cliff, I felt my palms sweating and my heart racing. I peered over the edge as a sense of unease gripped my stomach. I had never rappelled down a cliff before, and this was dizzying! Rappelling is descending a rock face backwards by walking your feet down the cliff, secured by a harness, ropes, and a person known as a belayer. As I prepared for my first rappel, the cliff face seemed like it was hundreds of feet down—it was actually about twenty feet. But I wasn't thinking. I was feeling, and the feeling was terror.

"You can do this!" I heard as I approached the first terrifying step. Gordon, my instructor, held my rope securely so that if I fell, he would catch me. I wasn't so sure. Later I learned that the phrase "You can do this!" is the siren call of Outward Bound. Virtually every instructor uses this phrase, and virtually every student comes to a point in his or her adventuring when they reach the end of their comfort zone and need to hear, "You can do this!" That day was the end of my comfort zone.

As the phrase echoed in my ear, I wasn't sure I would actually be able to make my body go over the edge of that cliff. A guy like me, with a distinct fear of heights, was no match for a mountain with a sheer drop-off. No, thank you. *Could I do this? Did I even want to do this?*

"This rope could lift a Volkswagen into the air, Paul. You're going to be fine," Gordon reassured me as he slid my rappel rope through a light metal contraption.

Everything was in place as I grabbed the rope. I paused and took it all in—the fear, the adrenaline, and the view.

Turning my back toward the drop-off, I heard, "Lean back and place your boots directly against the rock wall." I felt my heart pound and my face flush. With great trepidation, I shifted the weight of the back side of my body over the edge of the cliff and placed my boots on the vertical wall of rock.

"Take a step down and let the rope slide," Gordon coached.

I did as Gordon instructed and slowly stepped backward, as if walking vertically backward down the side of the rock. Then another step. I began to watch the rock face change in front of me, and I looked down to see my rope slide smoothly at my side. I tried not to look past my harness, for fear I'd recognize the ever-so-distant ground beneath me and lose my wits.

Each backward step took me closer to the ground, my safe haven. As the rope slid through my clammy hands, what had once been fear built into confidence. I was rappelling! Sooner than I was ready for it to be over, I was on the ground looking up the rock face. Wow! I had done it. I never thought someone with a fear of heights could walk backward down the side of a mountain and live to tell about it. I had always been too terrified to get close to doing anything like this before, but I did it! What an exhilarating feeling!

Looking back, I know this experience was about way more than just moving my teenage body down a twenty-foot descent. It was about taking myself outside of my comfort zone in the context of safe support so that I could build confidence to face other seemingly impossible areas of my life. And it worked! My sense of self-efficacy—the feeling that I could accomplish hard things—skyrocketed after this rappel. I whipped around, clapping my hands, ready to face the next big challenge. Nothing could stop me now.

Adventure I Never Imagined

I was ready for a summer of adventure when I signed up to work at that camp in Steamboat Springs, Colorado, the summer of 1968, but I was totally unprepared for rappelling. In fact, I was unprepared for most of the opportunities that came at me that summer. But, piece by piece, the summer unfolded, metamorphosing me from a boy into a man.

Eighteen years old and excited to help, I had arrived in May to prepare the camp for the teens who were soon to arrive. Almost immediately I learned that one of the leaders in the outdoor adventure program had gotten sick and could not come that summer. Gordon Brown asked me if I could help co-lead the wilderness excursions for a small group of students. Thinking it sounded fun, I jumped at the opportunity. Little did I know that I was signing up for an experience that would simultaneously force me to face way too many of my fears and mature me into a responsible human being. What they didn't tell me was that I would head off to college four months later with more initiative and fire in my belly than ever before in my life.

The program was called Outward Bound. It is a program for teenagers that provides adventure to help them learn three crucial attitudes:

1. An appreciation for the wilderness,

2. Teamwork,

3. Greater self-confidence by doing things that the students never thought they could achieve.

The motto of Outward Bound is "To Serve, to Strive and Not to Yield." This comes from the poem "Ulysses" by Alfred, Lord Tennyson. Lines sixty-five through seventy:

Tho' much is taken, much abides; and tho'
We are not now that strength which in old days
Moved earth and heaven, that which we are, we are;
One equal temper of heroic hearts,
Made weak by time and fate, but strong in will
To strive, to seek, to find, and not to yield.

That summer with Outward Bound was all about servant leadership. Before the students arrived, I had to experience every physical and psychological challenge for myself in leader training. Then I would be ready to protect the lives of the students I would lead. Luckily, I had three other rookies alongside me, going through the same torturous and exciting training to become patrol instructors that summer.

What Gordon Brown Taught Me

First, Gordon Brown, our mentor and a certified Colorado Outward Bound Master Instructor, took us to the mountains. That's when I experienced that terrifying rappel I detailed earlier. After I had rappelled, the fear was gone, and I dove into the opportunity to learn how to "belay" others down the rock face. To "belay" someone means to be an anchor for them and hold them steady with a rope in case they fall on the way up or down a rock face. I loved the simultaneous exposure to fear and sense of security that I had the honor of providing for others as a guide.

Perhaps this informed my leadership style going forward because, to this day, I love encouraging people to step out of their comfort zones within the safety of good leadership and great faith in God.

Next, Gordon took us to the Yampa River, which runs through Steamboat Springs. We rookies donned swim gear, life jackets, and helmets. We grabbed our paddles and slid into our individual kayaks. I snickered as I snapped on my helmet. It seemed a bit excessive to need a helmet in mild water. But, as the five of us paddled down the river, I heard and saw the whitewater raging in the distance. *Oh boy!* I thought. This was going to be fun and wet! Together, we bounced through rapid after rapid and made it through safely to the other side. Gordon taught us how to kayak, flip, and recover in the kayak again.

That's when it was our turn to practice while Gordon watched. As he stood observing, I neared a particularly rushing rapid. Bouncing side to side against each cascade of water, I maneuvered my kayak methodically and managed to stay upright. Boom! I was so proud of myself that I turned to look back at the heart-stopping rapids I had just conquered. With a cheer of pride, I raised my paddle in victory. And suddenly, I flipped.

Though I was in calmer water, my kayak continued downstream, with my head underwater, bouncing along the rocks on the bottom of the Yampa. Thank you, Gordon, for insisting we wear helmets! I flipped back over, just as my training had taught me to do. After that, I never sneered at the advice of my leader again. When he told me to bring something, or wear something, or do something, I readily took his word for it. He knew what I would need, so I trusted him.

After our water training, we went on an expedition to hike along the Continental Divide through the rolling meadows at ten thousand feet. I had never seen views that gorgeous in my life. I tried to keep my focus on my compass and map, in case Gordon asked me to take a turn navigating my way through the wilderness. As we found our way to camp the first night, it began to pour rain. Instead of moping under the discomfort of a cold and wet night, Gordon taught us to light fires in the rain. We learned how to camp without leaving a trace, how to cook a delicious, hot supper over the fire, and how to stay dry in thunderstorms that last for days. Then we sat quietly and took in the beauty all around us. This transformational adventure was not for the faint of heart, though. In the following days, we ended up hiking fifty miles along the Continental Divide.

Because there was snow at the top, Gordon taught us how to snow climb and glissade. A glissade is a controlled slide (sometimes not so controlled) on your feet down a snowy slope without skis. That summer, I learned to fall in love with the wilderness and the way it refreshes my spirit.

From rappelling to whitewater kayaking to glissading and more, the beginning of the summer of 1968 prepared me to be the man and leader I wanted to be for the rest of my life. Yes, I learned many outdoor survival skills. I also learned that I could do far more than I ever thought possible. I learned to stay calm and focused during emergencies. But the most important thing I learned was how to serve others by helping them do more than they thought possible. I learned the importance of keeping them safe, and I learned to replicate myself as a leader by training others to train others.

Great Leaders Lead by Example

I learned all this by observing Gordon Brown. Gordon Brown truly led by example. Every activity and challenge we were expected to perform, he did first, in front of us. He showed us the way, taught us how to do it safely, then had us do it in front of him until we got it right. Then we did it again…and again. I learned later in life that this is the essence of Christian discipleship: show someone the way, practice with safety and support, and equip them to take steps forward on their own. Then encourage them to disciple others.

At the end of this training, I was equipped physically and mentally to be the kind of leader my students would need in the wilderness. Gordon taught me to serve others, to care for others, to make wise decisions for the benefit of the group, and to stay calm and focused during emergencies. Thank you, Gordon, for these immeasurably great life and leadership skills!

Why was Gordon so thorough? The precious lives of young people would be in our care. We had to know what we were doing. We couldn't risk their lives through our lack of training. We had to train them like we were trained. These lessons informed the way Dynamic Church

Planting International (DCPI) trains church planters. I never want to send someone out into the world unequipped to face the dangers of church planting. That is why we are careful to equip the precious people God brings to us: so they can follow boldly wherever God leads them, ready to thrive no matter what comes.

Leading Like a Wilderness Scout

That summer was my true leadership launching point. That's when I learned that leadership is a process of encouraging people to do more than they ever thought possible. It's also a commitment to keep those you lead safe. As I assumed leadership positions in the future, I continued to have opportunities to live out what I learned that summer as an Outward Bound Instructor.

Step by step we trained, modeled, and empowered those in our patrols, or groups, to take risks, enjoy adventures, and feel the exhilaration and pride of overcoming their fears.

The Influence of Outward Bound

Outward Bound is an international network of outdoor education organizations that was founded in the United Kingdom by Kurt Hahn and Lawrence Holt in 1941. Today there are organizations, called schools, in thirty-three countries that are attended by more than 250,000 people each year.

Kurt Hahn was raised as a Jew and converted to Christianity and preached in the Church of Scotland later in life.

Professor Hahn founded Gordonstoun School in 1934, which is where father and son Prince Philip and Prince Charles of England were educated. The principles from Gordonstoun flowed into Outward Bound.

This organization helped to shape the US Peace Corps and numerous other outdoor adventure programs. Its aim is to foster the personal growth and social skills of participants by using challenging expeditions in the outdoors.

Outward Bound's founding mission was to improve the survival chances of young seamen in World War II after their ships were torpedoed in the mid-Atlantic. It did just that.

Because of my personal transformation through Outward Bound, I started an Outward Bound program at my college a few summers later. Equipped by Gordon himself, I was now the Master Instructor, responsible for training and equipping other instructors at my campus. I oversaw them as they led their students. Just like Gordon Brown did for me.

Saving Molly

I specifically remember an instructor named Molly. She had a big smile, a big laugh, and a great attitude. One day, we were in the mountains of Colorado, and it was cold—around thirty-five degrees Fahrenheit. Rain had fallen for a couple of days, and we began to notice a change in Molly. She seemed different than her usual vivacious self. She was shivering. Her speech was slurred. She acted clumsy and confused.

We diagnosed the problem: hypothermia. Hypothermia can lead to death if not addressed immediately. So, we stopped our expedition and rapidly constructed a water-resistant lean-to, which is like a tent without the walls. Then we zipped two sleeping bags together and laid them down on a pad. The fastest and safest cure for hypothermia is body heat. Molly got into the sleeping bag and removed all outer clothing, leaving her in her underwear. Two others did the same and used their body heat—one on each side—to help Molly's body regain its homeostasis. She recovered well and quickly. Thanks to Gordon Brown, I knew what this was and what to do, and everything worked out fine for Molly.

Leading my students meant serving them and doing everything in my power to protect their lives. When Molly had a problem, we stopped everything to help her. Her needs became my highest priority. The idea that leadership is a top-down phenomenon is so wrong. The greatest leaders aren't about themselves. They are about taking care of their people and drawing out the best in them by providing growing experiences in the context of compassionate support. One thing I learned that summer was that if I was going to be a good leader, I was going to have to be a good servant.

You Can Do This

Whatever your leadership experience, I want you to know that you can do far more than you think you can do. Whether you're accustomed to risking your life in the wilderness or you're used to safer situations, I bet you have learned a thing or two about leadership over the years, and I bet, even though you have learned a lot, you will still come across leadership situations in your future that baffle and stall you. So, what do you do?

First, you rely on your training. I believe the best training in wisdom is God's Word. When you are without direction and needing guidance as a leader, turn to Proverbs and read. Ask God to speak to you and give you wisdom to know what's best for your team.

Second, stay calm and put the needs of others first. As you serve others, you are leading the way that Jesus Christ led his disciples. When you care about them and keep them safe, you are equipping them to take risks and charge forward with great confidence and expectation for what God will do in their lives. This has very little to do with you and much more to do with God's working in their lives, so serve them and watch what God does.

Third, persevere. Remember, "I can do all things through him who strengthens me" (Philippians 4:13 ESV).

When you're tired, stalled out, or about to give up, remember that you can be content in any circumstance because God gives you strength. Go in his strength and grace, and, whatever you do, do not yield!

LIFE LESSONS

- "You can do it!" One of the most powerful things you can do for someone you lead is to call them to do more than they thought possible and to support them as they accomplish their challenges. This will build their confidence and capacity. Step by step train, model, and empower those on your team to take risks, enjoy adventures, and feel the exhilaration and pride of overcoming their fears.

- Learn and teach skills for a lifetime. What skills can you teach others? Learn to stay calm and focused during emergencies. Learn how to replicate yourself in other leaders as you train others to train others. See 2 Timothy 2:2.

- As a leader, your priority is serving others. As you serve others, you are leading the way that Jesus Christ led his disciples. When you care about them and keep them safe, you are equipping them to take risks and charge forward with great confidence and expectation for what God will do in their lives. See Matthew 20:28.

WHAT ABOUT YOU?

1. "To serve, to strive and not to yield." This comes from the poem "Ulysses" by Alfred, Lord Tennyson. Ulysses and his men are twenty years older than when they went to war. They don't have the strength and vitality they used to have. There is not a lot of gas in the tank. Even though they are old and broken, they still have the dedication to serve others and keep moving forward. They refuse to give up. These guys are a team with one heartbeat. What is one way you can apply "to serve, to strive and not to yield" to your life? How can you influence those in your life to serve, to strive and not to yield?

2. What are the experiences or challenges that terrify you? How do you deal with them? Do you avoid them? Do you overcome them? How?

3. What is one experience that you think is something you could never do, and yet, you are drawn to this experience? How can you get the help you need to do it? What will it take for you to do something that is far beyond what you think you can accomplish?

4. My experiences in the wilderness, in the mountains, and in the ocean have taught me that God made me to experience him and to worship him and to listen to him

in the wild places. What do you think and feel about this? Would you like to learn to have a conversation with God in the outdoors?

5. Gordon Brown demonstrated the essentials of discipleship. What are they? How can you become a more effective disciple-making disciple?

6

TO QUIT OR NOT TO QUIT

"If the horse is dead, get off."

—AMERICAN INDIAN SAYING

"Never give in, never give in, never, never, never, never..."

—WINSTON CHURCHILL

I love adventure. I wanted to take people with me on every adventure, to get them outdoors and invite them to exceed their personal limits, so I launched a program at my college called NATURE. The NATURE program was based on my Outward Bound training in Colorado. The plan was for me to select nine students to join me on three life-changing and arduous expeditions in the Smoky Mountains, in the Everglades, and on a wild Florida coastal island.

Our first NATURE meeting drew fifty students, more than 10 percent of my small college's population. I excitedly outlined the expeditions awaiting us and described how tough they were going to be. This narrowed those interested to thirty-four students. Of those thirty-four, nine were chosen to join the expeditions.

Rain in the Smoky Mountains

The nine students plus me drove north from Florida to the Great Smoky Mountains in Tennessee. This is my favorite mountain range in the eastern part of the United States. More different kinds of plants and trees live here than in any part of the eastern United States. Sometimes there is a natural blue fog that hangs over the valleys. This is where the range gets its name: the Smokies.

The Smokies looked particularly beautiful at the start of our first expedition. I was thrilled to share this exciting place with our nine students. As we started our march, I hoped that these students would disregard the bone-chilling rain dripping through the trees onto us and concentrate on the beautiful adventure that lay ahead.

Here is an excerpt from my journal of the experience:

It has rained for two days and nights since we left the trailhead of the Appalachian Trail at Clingman's Dome. We stopped at log huts early both afternoons to get some hot food in us and to dry our clothes.

The damp, cold clothing on our backs was beginning to weigh us down. As we slogged through the depressing landscape, the inhospitable rain, mud, and gray skies tempted a few group members to quit. The first to give up was a student named Debby.

Though Debby was a natural leader, strong and capable, she was reaching the end of her strength by the end of day one. But she couldn't stop then. We were at least a two-day hike to the nearest town. She would need to press on with us for two more days. We hoped the rain would let up, but the opposite happened. The rain relentlessly poured, with thunder overhead, and the trail became a stream. Debby was listless. There was no light in her eyes. I could tell her body and spirit were depleted.

Later I wrote in my journal:

> As we climb Thunderhead Mountain, Debby is failing. Her labored footsteps are only a foot long. Finally, she just laid down on the uphill trail in the rain. I gave her more woolen clothing, placed her pack on my back, stepped behind her, and pushed her up the mountain.

She insisted that she just wanted to lie down and that we could send someone back for her. I knew we couldn't do that; she would die of hypothermia. So, we toiled our way toward Cade's Cove, where we found a motel for Debby that was close to a bus station to take her back home.

To Quit...

Debby did not go on the other two NATURE expeditions with us. Though I think she probably could have persevered through the rest of our Appalachian Trail hike, I'm not sure it would have been good for her health. When your health is at risk for the sake of the adventure, it's best to choose your health over the adventure.

Perseverance is important, and in God's strength you can persevere through anything. But sometimes, when asking the question "To quit or not to quit?" the answer is "Yes, quit."

Consider this picture: An American Indian is riding his horse out on the great western plains of the USA. Suddenly, the horse dies and falls to the ground. Should the man stay mounted on the animal? Of course not. He should get off.

From this scenario comes the old American Indian saying: "When the horse is dead, get off!"

Sometimes in adventure and in life, you reach a point when you recognize that the path you're on isn't going anywhere good. *That* may be a sign that you've got a dead horse. When you realize you're riding a dead horse, *that's* when you quit.

My Dead Horses

When I first went to college, I was determined to become a marine biologist. I had done well in math and science in high school, which were requirements for this degree. I even led the creation and placement of an artificial reef into the ocean during my first independent study project in college.

Then, in my studies, I ran into calculus. In high school, I had done well in algebra and trigonometry, but I just could not understand calculus in college. It just wasn't in me. Without calculus, I could not major in marine biology. My horse named calculus died, and I just had to get off and continue to pursue my future elsewhere, not in marine biology.

The same thing happened when I was three years into planting my first church. One night, I awoke from a terrifying dream. I realized that I had no vision for this church after January of the following year. There was just an impenetrable blackness ahead. For me, a visionary leader, to have lost God's vision for the organization I was leading terrified me.

I will get into this more in my next book, but for now, I want to say that I never want to do ministry without vision. So, when I sought the Lord about this, he made it clear the Holy Spirit was moving me on to my next ministry. The church, thankfully, continued for decades, and I was freed up by the Holy Spirit to do what God called me to do. This dead horse was God's way of redirecting my path toward his next season for me.

Debby went on to pursue her own independent study projects that aligned with her interests and health. For her, quitting was how God redirected her path toward other adventures. Though I believe firmly in perseverance, sometimes quitting a dead horse can be a powerful redirection in your life.

How Do You Recognize a Dead Horse?

A dead horse might look like a program, a relationship, a job, or a project that shows no sign of life. It often takes time to recognize that the horse is dead, so we may keep going, though we are stuck in ineffectiveness.

Dr. Ron Johnson writes,

> "Discerning our dead horses takes uncommon wisdom, and rarely happens without an intentional process. Perhaps such discernment begins with noticing, not denying, a lack of forward movement. (Others of us must absolutely crash!) The discernment continues as we discover that despite trying harder, or smarter, or more aggressively, we remain at the same place."[2]

If there is something in your life that is stuck and not moving, and no matter how hard you try, it just doesn't work, that might be a dead horse. Don't be tempted to make the horse move again by buying a stronger whip or asking others how they ride dead horses. If the horse truly isn't moving, just get off and do something different.

Yes, the Christian life is a life of perseverance. It's a life of choosing not to quit as we follow Christ. But it's also a life of listening to God's direction and recognizing when the Holy Spirit is using a dead horse to redirect our lives.

Maybe this is a breakup of a relationship that needs to happen.

---

2   Ron Johnson, PhD, "Dismounting Dead Horses: A Metaphor for Change," Explore Faith, http://www.explorefaith.org/lifelines_horses.html.

Maybe this is a job change that needs to happen. Maybe this is a project that needs to be stopped. Maybe this is a purchase that needs to be returned or sold. Whatever your dead horse, the first step toward finding God's best for your next phase of life is getting off the horse. Sometimes when asking *to quit or not to quit*, the answer is *quit*.

For those who are afraid to dismount a dead horse because you've already invested so much into it: I promise, if you dismount this horse, God will rebuild in more beautiful ways than you can imagine. This will be a pivotal moment where God redirects you to something much better than you had envisioned for yourself because he loves you.

For those who find it difficult to dismount a dead horse because quitting makes you feel like a failure: if you never fail, you probably are not taking risks. Failure will lead to personal growth or innovation in your life or in your organization. John Wooden, the legendary basketball coach, said it best: "Failure is not fatal, but failure to change might be." Dismounting a dead horse might be the best thing you choose to do in this season of your life.

Every situation presents you the opportunity to quit or not to quit. When you spot a dead horse, get off, stand to your feet, and ask, "What's next, God?" and go on to fulfill God's purpose for your life.

...Or Not to Quit

While Debby quit for the sake of her health, another student named Claire persevered and succeeded. Though I initially thought of her as small and meek, Claire was mighty like a lion on the inside! Her demeanor grew stronger and more joyful the longer we hiked. I remember her face, smiling, with the rain dripping off her cap. She hiked powerfully up Thunderhead Mountain despite the downpour.

At the end of this NATURE expedition, Claire said, "This encounter taught me that I can be strong. It was the best thing I have ever done in my life."

Exploring the Everglades

Our NATURE program went on two other excursions together that year. Both excursions took us to our limits, where each of us had to decide *to quit or not to quit*. The next excursion included a wild boar chase on a deserted island off the coast of Florida, and after that, we adventured in the Everglades.

The Florida Everglades is like a river that is eighty miles wide and only a few inches deep, flowing southward from Lake Okeechobee, covering most of south Florida. The Everglades is a unique ecosystem of low, swampy land with tall, flowing grass and countless branching waterways. There are only two Everglades on our planet: one is in Australia along the Noosa River, and the other is in south Florida, in the United States.

As we wrapped up our first day of exploring the Everglades by canoe, the wind began to pick up. What started as mildly choppy water became tumultuous and extremely dangerous as we canoed against the wind and waves to make it back to our bay, where our campsite was set up. What should have been a pretty easy paddle was now somewhat impossible. The wind was blowing about twenty miles per hour and causing large waves to come at us.

The waves drove our canoes back and to the side, and all the sloshing water began to fill our canoes and swamp us. The most important maneuver was to keep our canoes pointed directly into the wind and waves so that we could stay headed in the right direction without tipping. If we allowed the wind and waves to turn our canoes broadside, they would capsize. We could find ourselves floating in that big bay.

Not even the best swimmer would be okay in waves like this. To make it worse, we were not the only creatures in the water. There were sharks and alligators that would love to eat us for lunch if our canoes dumped us out. Upright canoes were our only hope of survival.

Earlier that day, as we had paddled through the shallow water and the mangrove trees on the way to the bay, we could see the gators' eyes just above the surface of the water. Along with beady eyes peering at us, their terrible snouts stuck up out of the water, as if they could smell the uneasiness radiating off the nine of us.

In my experience, there are some adventures that crank up the adrenaline for the fun of it—skydiving, cliff jumping, rappelling, and usually scuba diving. But this moment had us all on edge because of the sheer danger—and most likely stupidity—of it. The question of *to quit or not to quit* was really no question at all in this moment. Though all of us wanted to quit, the question was really *to die or not to die*. Our choice was not to die, so we kept paddling, battling the waves.

Exhausted both physically and mentally, we persevered for the better part of the afternoon and finally made it to our campsite. After eating a good dinner, we all collapsed into our beds knowing we had done something we didn't think we could do. We didn't quit. Though we were weary, we were proud conquerors. We were strengthened with the confidence we had built during the hardship.

A Midnight Paddle to the Gulf

A day later, we boarded our canoes again. This time, we went for a night paddle. We started out at ten at night and paddled down the Chatham River through islands of mangrove trees toward the Gulf of Mexico. In the moonlit night, we set our minds toward our beach destination. As we paddled by one island, we awoke a huge flock of white ibis birds, which exploded off the island and into the dark like an erupting volcano. Our canoeing must have frightened them into flying away en masse, and boy did they frighten us! That is, until we realized they were harmless.

With a sigh of relief, I realized that nearly every turn in life presents opportunities to quit or not to quit. Being scared can easily distract us from staying on course. Being exhausted can beckon us to give up. Being doubtful of our choice to walk on the wild side can cause us to want to turn back. But sometimes, just when you think you should quit, you open your eyes, and there before you is something unexpectedly rare, beautiful, or significant that makes you take the next step forward.

Right then, our river emerged into the Gulf of Mexico. At midnight, the moon was above the horizon in front of us. It glittered on the sets of waves breaking in from the Gulf. This was one of those glorious natural moments that God has imprinted upon my mind. I realized how very privileged I was to witness this display of utter beauty. The beauty of this sight sang over us: "All that struggle was worth it! Look where you are now!"

You Can Do Anything

Though I wasn't a Christian at the time, I now see that moments of grace that arrive while you are tempted to quit are God's way of calling you to persevere. When you are in God's will, walking forward by faith, challenges still come at you. But God's grace comes at you more sweetly and powerfully, reminding your soul to stay the course.

The apostle Paul said in Philippians 4:13 MSG, "Whatever I have, wherever I am, I can make it through anything in the One who makes me who I am."

In the New International Version, Philippians 4:13 says: "I can do all this through him who gives me strength."

On a planet filled with God's glory, there are unlimited opportunities to witness him every day. Even in the midst of the mundane, God is present. Even in the midst of hardship, God is shaping us. Even in the midst of confusion or loss, God speaks. We can't determine what will happen to us in this life, but because of him, we can persevere whenever he calls us to keep going.

The Reward for Not Quitting

I have noticed, over the years, that those who choose not to quit gain a whole new sense of self. The badge they earn at the end of hardship is confidence and self-efficacy. When you choose to persevere in the face of hard times, you discover that you can, in fact, do hard things, which changes every situation from then on. As the Lord leads you, and you walk on the wild side by faith, persevere toward your goal whenever possible. You can do all things through Christ who strengthens you.

LIFE LESSONS

- We can't determine what will happen to us in this life. We can determine how we will respond to it: either by giving up or persevering. When it is terribly hard to keep going in a project or a challenge, ask the Lord to reveal to you whether you should persevere or "get off the dead horse."
- If God calls you to persevere, then keep on keeping on. See Philippians 4:13.
- If God calls you to move on in your life and ministry, then move on toward your destiny in him! Purposefully abandon projects and processes that have outlived their usefulness. Embrace the future!
- If you have to choose between your health (physical or mental) and your adventure, choose your health.
- Stay focused on what you need to do during stressful times. Keep your canoe and your life pointed directly into the wind and the waves so that you don't capsize.
- Seek and experience moments of incredible natural beauty, like the wild beach in the Everglades at midnight with the full moon shining on the breakers.

WHAT ABOUT YOU?

1. Can you remember doing something that you never thought you had the ability to do? How did that make you feel about yourself?

2. In your life, what is an incredibly beautiful moment in nature you have experienced? What was it like? What did it teach you about God or yourself?

3. Why do you think nature is so crucial to helping us sustain our strength and perspective on life?

4. Can you remember a situation when you quit and wished that you had persevered? Can you remember another situation in which you persevered and are so glad you did?

5. Can you remember a situation in which you continued to "ride a dead horse" and wished you had gotten off much earlier?

6. How can you discern when to persevere and when to "get off the dead horse"? Here are some ideas:
   - You could take a prayer retreat and ask God to give you wisdom. (I have written a book about how to have an effective prayer retreat, called *The Prayer Retreat Profile* by Paul Becker. Check it out on Amazon.)
   - You could go to your mentors and ask for their guidance.
   - You could seek and listen to the leading of the Holy Spirit.
   - What else can you do?
   - What will you do?
   - How can you make this a healthy decision-making process that you follow for the rest of your life?

7

MEETING GOD
IN MICA BASIN

"God opposes the proud but shows favor to the humble."

–JAMES 4:6B

"God reveals himself unfailingly to the thoughtful seeker."

–HONORE DE BALZAC

I f you have never been to Mica Basin, Colorado, I recommend planning your next hike there! It is the most beautiful place I have ever experienced, and I have seen a lot of places over my years. Mica Basin is north of Steamboat Springs, Colorado, a few miles west of the Continental Divide, and just a few miles south of the Wyoming border. Because of its location in Northern Colorado and its elevation of over ten thousand feet, Mica Basin is filled with snow for nine months of the year, and there are avalanche cirques in the basin's mountains.

Mica Basin is a bowl-shaped valley surrounded by steep-walled mountains on three sides. Mica Lake sits in the middle of the basin, endowed each year with water from the snowmelt flowing down the mountainsides. Flowing out of Mica Lake is meandering Mica Creek, cascading in places and glassily tranquil in others. In the summer months, the basin sings with wildflowers bursting to life, elk setting foot in the lake for a drink, and fallen trees giving way to young, thriving trees, brimming with leaves and the finest of outdoor aromas.

In my last chapter, I shared with you about Outward Bound and its impact on my life. It is a global outdoor program that helps people appreciate nature, work together as a group, and become convinced that they can do more than they ever thought possible. I served as an Outward Bound Instructor in my late teens and mid-twenties. As a result, I spent a lot of time in Mica Basin and led many backpacking trips here. Though I was very familiar with the terrain, one group hike opened my eyes to what I really didn't know and changed my life forever.

Hiking with Danny

In the spring of 1976, I was leading a group of eight young people, along with my co-instructor, uphill along the Mica Creek trail. This was part of a fifty-mile backpacking trip along the Continental Divide. In the front of the group was a young man named Danny, who was fifteen years old and a natural-born leader. I was leading from the rear, making sure the nine of us were all good and moving forward.

Danny would hike quickly, then look back at the rest of us slow-movers with disdain on his face. He hadn't learned yet that any group can only hike as quickly as its slowest hiker. He kept urging us on and grew a bit disgusted with us because we weren't hiking at his pace. Sometimes he was so far in front of us, I wondered if he felt like he was a part of our group at all.

This can happen to leaders who aren't careful. They are so far in front of their people with their ideas and pace that the people wonder if the leader is still a part of the team. More on this in the second book of this trilogy.

It was early spring, which meant there was still a load of snow in the mountains of Colorado. It was melting, so the snow was dense and we could walk on top without much "post-holing." The creek was stunning as we climbed up on its bank. The water rushed down the stream bed through trees and branches and over the rocks and around the mounds of snow. Surrounded by beauty, our team pressed upward on this intense hike. We wore gaiters over our pants to keep the snow and the water out of our boots. We had heavy packs on our backs, containing the supplies we needed to camp. It was a few hours before we reached 10,400 feet and Mica Lake.

Finally, we were able to see the little lake in the center of the basin. The banks of the lake were free of pine trees, and snow surrounded it like sand on a seashore. The pristine blue lake stood out against the snowy background like a dazzling blue sapphire on a white sweater. It was gorgeous!

As we kept hiking to our camp, we could see the slopes sweep upward from the lake on three sides, each covered in snow and ice. The jagged mountain peaks formed a semicircle above us. Little Agnes Mountain was to the left and Big Agnes Mountain, at over twelve thousand feet, was to the right. I love climbing mountains, though I know not everyone enjoys it as I do. Climbing mountains makes me feel alive, and I loved sharing that with others through Outward Bound.

We found our site in the trees just below and made camp. Danny was great at telling people what to do. His teammates weren't so great at listening to him, which was another frustration for Danny. We put up the tarps and laid out our sleeping bags on our mats. A couple of us started gathering wood (this was many years ago when you could still burn wood in the wilderness). Two of us set the fire and cooked our dinner. The food tasted wonderful in the cool of the early evening.

Dusk turned to dark, and our team of eight gathered around the fire. As the fire flickered, we talked about the next morning and the rock climbing and rappelling we would do, excited by the challenge. In a quiet voice that shook just a little, Julie, a seventeen-year-old city girl, said, "I'm terrified of heights. I don't think I'll join you for the climb and rappel tomorrow." As a leader, I listened to her concerns and reassured her that whatever happened tomorrow, we would do it safely.

Rappelling and Belaying

The next day after breakfast, we gathered our climbing gear and hiked up the snow slope to the bottom of a pinnacle of rock below Little Agnes Mountain. This was our rock-climbing site. Maddie, another Outward Bound Instructor, and I instructed each team member how to wear climbing harnesses correctly. She and I carefully tested each one.

Then Maddie and I trained our team in climbing, rappelling, and belaying. Rappelling is descending a rock face by using a rope coiled around the body and fixed at a higher point. Belaying is securing the rope at the top or bottom of the climb and holding the rope to help control the descent for the rappeller. The belayer should keep the rope locked off with the rope wrapped around his body and his hand tight up against his stomach whenever the climber is not moving. As the climber moves on the climb, the belayer must make sure that the climber has the right amount of rope by paying out or pulling in excess rope.

I made the first climb. The first climber has no one above to belay him, so someone must belay from the ground. Maddie belayed me, and I set up protection as I went up the face about one hundred feet. I reached the top and anchored the coil of climbing rope that I had been carrying around my neck to a boulder at the top. I threw the rest of the rope down the pinnacle and found a secure belaying spot to sit where I could use my legs to push against the rock.

When I had anchored myself to that spot and got in position, I called down, "On belay." The first volunteer to climb was…you guessed it…Danny. Maddie secured Danny to the rope by attaching it to his harness. He called out, "Climbing!" And he climbed easily to the top.

I released him from the rope and placed him in the belay position, anchoring him in and giving him a little refresher on how to belay. He assured me that was not necessary, that he knew what he was doing. We threw the rope down. Maddie secured Julie to the rope. Julie was crying and saying, "I'm just too scared…I can't do this…I'm going to fall!" Maddie was reassuring her and encouraging her using the Outward Bound watchwords: "You can do it!"

Danny called down, "On belay." Julie, through her tears, called up, "Climbing." She began to climb. Danny was pulling in the excess rope when, suddenly, the rope was rapidly going the other direction. We heard a cry from Julie below. Julie was falling. Danny didn't stop the rope! Instead, he looked at me quizzically. The rope was just whizzing around his waist and down the side of the mountain. I reached over quickly and stopped the rope.

I called down, "Julie, are you okay?"

All I could hear was Julie crying.

Maddie called up, "She fell about ten feet. Let me check."

Danny payed out the rope as Julie went to the bottom of the climb, where she was unhooked from the rope and evaluated by Maddie.

Maddie called up, "Julie is fine. Just shaken up with a few scrapes."

Danny was distraught. He realized that he had Julie's life in his hands as her belayer and he had failed to do his job. He didn't keep her safe. He was letting her life slip through his hands by not stopping the rope.

I took over as the belayer. All the students successfully climbed the pinnacle. Even Julie got back on the rope and made it all the way to the top. I was so proud of her for overcoming her fear! Each one made a winning rappel down.

Awestruck by Beauty

We paused for a moment, and I had time to look around. This truly was the most beautiful place I had ever seen. I breathed in the perfection.

Suddenly, I thought of the manmade world. I considered a typical city, which, over time, becomes slums of aging buildings and abandoned trash. The landscape in Mica Basin was strikingly different from anything a human could create.

Mica Basin was ancient. Yet, its perfection never changed with time. In that moment my eyes were opened, and I just knew that there had to be a God. He must have touched our world in a personal way to make and maintain something so stunning. He must be active still in the world because he cared to keep this place so beautiful for us to see. There was no way this was an accident. He must be truly amazing because he makes his creation so perfect.

Right in front of my group of students, I fell to my knees and worshipped God. I was no longer an agnostic—one who didn't know God. All of a sudden, I was open to God. I believed in a God who touched the earth and was involved with mankind. I wasn't a Christian yet; that would come later. But I was definitely someone who respected the hugeness and beauty of God. I knew that God was real and involved with our world and our lives.

This passage of Scripture, too, came later, but it perfectly describes what I experienced in Mica Basin that day:

> *"For since the creation of the world God's invisible qualities—his eternal power and divine nature—have been clearly seen, being understood from what has been made, so that people are without excuse."* (Romans 1:20)

I saw God, his power and divinity, in what he had made—this wonderful place called Mica Basin.

Humbled

Later that night, around the campfire in Mica Basin, I witnessed a transformation in another person as well. Danny was broken because he had failed to protect Julie during her climb. He wept and humbled himself and asked for her forgiveness. She forgave him. From that day until the end of the expedition, Danny was a different leader. He led from behind so that he could take care of the team. He wasn't perfect, but he was more patient and encouraging.

"God opposes the proud but shows favor to the humble."
(James 4:6b)

Danny began to learn this lesson in Mica Basin.

At the beginning of our time together, Danny reminded me of me at his age: proud, selfish, ignoring others' needs, going to the front, setting the pace, and leaving others behind.

This excursion in the Mica Basin helped change that for Danny. For me, the Mica Basin opened my eyes and softened my heart to a God who loved me.

LIFE LESSONS

- Experience God through the wonder of his creation by moving through it: hiking, climbing, surfing, diving, running, biking, gardening, golfing, or your favorite activity. God wants to reveal himself to you. See Romans 1:20.
- God opposes the proud but shows favor to the humble who serve others. See James 4:6.

WHAT ABOUT YOU?

1. Have you ever really let someone down, like Danny did? What did that feel like for you? For that person? Did that person forgive you? What lessons did you learn from this experience?

2. Have you seen in the lives of others how God opposes the proud but shows favor to the humble who serve others? Who is your best example? Have you experienced this in your life? What is your takeaway?

3. Has God become real to you? How did this happen? Have you written down your story? Have you shared this story with others?

4. What is your most beautiful place on earth? Whom do you need to take there?

8

THE "SOLO" WEEKEND THAT CHANGED EVERYTHING

"For God so loved the world that he gave his one and only Son, that whoever believes in him shall not perish but have eternal life."

–JOHN 3:16

In my early twenties, I co-led an outdoor program in Butler, Pennsylvania, where we took juvenile delinquents on wilderness adventures to teach them to be disciplined, law-abiding citizens. Our target group was young men between the ages of fifteen and eighteen. There were some real criminals in our program, including young people from Pittsburgh and Philadelphia who were armed robbers and those who had committed assault. They sounded fierce, but I was not afraid to be with them. They responded well to love, encouragement, and care.

The major advantage for the young people who graduated from our twenty-four-day program was that they would be free to return home. Rather than serving another year or two in a youth detention center (otherwise known as jail), when they completed our program, their sentence was completed. Why? Because the leaders of the youth detention center believed that, if an offender graduated from a demanding, disciplined outdoor program, they had acquired the skills and attitudes needed to live as an upstanding citizen.

Going "Solo"

One of the disciplines we taught them was the "solo." A solo is a three-day, two-night period of alone time in the wilderness. The purpose of the solo is to develop self-awareness, self-confidence, and maturity.

On our way to our solo experience, our group traveled east into the Appalachian Mountains of Pennsylvania. We hiked into the wilderness together. Then I placed each student in his own private campsite. These campsites were off the main trail, far enough apart that the students could not see or hear one another. Each one knew where the main trail was and where I was camped, so if they had a serious problem they could find me. They had only minimal survival gear—a tarp to keep the rain away, a sleeping bag and pad, warm clothes, water, food, matches, and a writing pad and pen.

Coming out of the city, most of these students had never been truly alone in their entire lives. During those three days, I had several visits from students who were frightened in the mountains. Fear of being alone and fear of the unknown unsettled their hardened façades, making them confront their fears, process their thoughts, and discover more about themselves. In the end, each student made it the entire three days and two nights—a true accomplishment for each young man!

The powerful experiences we had over our twenty-four days with these students truly broke down their walls and recreated them into healthier, stronger, more balanced individuals, ready to contribute good things to our world. I am so proud of the criminal justice system for supporting this type of growth opportunity.

But there was one young man who did well at the beginning and started to fail as we neared the end of the course. His name was Julio. As graduation approached, Julio became rebellious and wouldn't complete the requirements of the program. When I and the other instructor talked to him, we realized that he really didn't *want* to complete the course. You see, Julio realized that if he was successful, he would return home. He didn't want to go home. Staying in the wilderness or in the youth detention center was much safer for him and offered less temptation. After all, his home and the streets of Philadelphia provided the environment that caused him to break the law in the first place. So, Julio purposefully failed the course.

My co-leader, Donna, and I worried about these young people when they returned home. Would they once again fall into a criminal lifestyle and wind up back in jail? I hoped not. I hoped that the time and experiences we had contributed to their lives would shape them for the better, forever.

My "Solo" in the City

Over the course of that program, I began to notice Donna as more than a friend. She was smart and strong. Competence has always been very attractive to me, and she was definitely capable. She had a bubbly, fun personality. It didn't hurt that she was a cute brunette, and we both enjoyed outdoor activities like cross-country skiing and backpacking.

Donna and I were becoming better friends. One day, I found some courage and asked her on a date. She replied that she was a Baptist and wouldn't date guys who weren't Christians.

Her answer shocked me. What could I say? I wasn't a Christian. I was open to God, but I was still agnostic.

"But…" Donna said—I found some hope in that one word—"if you will take my Bible and read Matthew, Mark, Luke, John, and Acts, we can talk."

From my Lutheran confirmation, I knew Donna was talking about the first five books of the New Testament. The first four books were all about Jesus coming to the earth and doing his work.

This sounded good to me. This was an easy price to pay. I would read these books on my next break from leading these excursions. I hoped that when I returned, after having read these five books from the Bible, she would say "Yes!" to a date.

Donna loaned me her Bible. Usually, I spent my break someplace peaceful, outdoors, and remote. This time, I was drawn to take my break in the city of Pittsburgh for three days and two nights. I decided to do a "solo in the city." I rented a room at Duquesne University. I wasn't attending the college, just renting a room. The university was located downtown, in the heart of Pittsburgh.

I had absolutely no expectation that the books of the Bible that Donna had asked me to read would make a difference in my life. I had already learned about the Bible during my Lutheran confirmation as a twelve-year-old. It hadn't stuck then, so why would it make a difference now? My one motivation was to meet this requirement with Donna so we could go out on a date. It was with that attitude that I started reading Matthew, then Mark, Luke, John, and finally Acts.

Surprises in the Bible

As I read about Jesus in the four gospels, I was shocked! The more I read, the more I became convicted that Jesus is who he said he was. This seemed like a miracle to me because I just wasn't expecting it.

God used verses like these to convict me about his Son, Jesus:

"Jesus performed many other signs in the presence of his disciples, which are not recorded in this book. But these are written that you may believe that Jesus is the Messiah, the Son of God, and that by believing you may have life in his name." (John 20:30–31)

I believed that Jesus was the Son of God in that room in Pittsburgh.

"The first thing Andrew did was to find his brother Simon and tell him, 'We have found the Messiah' (that is, the Christ)." (John 1:41)

I learned that Messiah and Christ both meant that Jesus was God's chosen one, the Savior. First for his people the Jews, and then for every one of us who would have faith in him.

"They said to the [Samaritan] woman, 'We no longer believe just because of what you said; now we have heard for ourselves, and we know that this man really is the Savior of the world.'" (John 4:42)

Yes, in that room in Duquesne University, I knew, for the first time, that Jesus truly was the Savior of the world.

"The disciples went and woke him, saying, 'Master, Master, we're going to drown!' He got up and rebuked the wind and the raging waters; the storm subsided, and all was calm." (Luke 8:24)

I saw that Jesus wasn't just the Savior of the world. He was God! He had power over wind and waves, so I realized I wanted him to be the Master, the Lord, the Boss of my life. If he had power over everything, I wanted him to have power in my life and lead me.

"I no longer call you servants, because a servant does not know his master's business. Instead, I have called you friends, for everything that I learned from my Father I have made known to you."
(John 15:15)

I found my heart whispering, "Thank you, Jesus, for being my friend."

"You call me 'Teacher' and 'Lord,' and rightly so, for that is what I am. Now that I, your Lord and Teacher, have washed your feet, you also should wash one another's feet." (John 13:13–14)

Then I saw that Jesus served those around him. He stirred my heart to want to serve others, too.

The last of the five books, Acts, was an adventure story of the early Christians as they shared Jesus and planted churches. These disciples traveled from Jerusalem to Antioch and then throughout the Mediterranean world, ending in Rome. It sounded like an adventure if I'd ever heard one—traveling to new countries, getting thrown in jail, meeting new people, sitting around fires on foreign islands, experiencing storms, shipwrecks, and snakebites, and on and on. I got totally onboard with the story.

That "solo" weekend, when I wasn't reading the Bible, I was walking through the slums of Pittsburgh, realizing how much people need Jesus the Savior.

Giving My Life to Jesus

I got back to my dorm room and began to pray, to simply speak, to a God who deeply loved me. I asked Jesus to be my Savior and to wash away my sins. I pledged my life to serve Jesus, the Son of God and the Master of my life. No one was there to persuade me. I had no fancy debates or emotional preachers calling me to repent. The weekend was quiet—just me and the Bible and my God who called me deeply and truly to follow him that weekend. I believed. From that weekend in Pittsburgh until today, Jesus has been with me.

"And surely I am with you always, to the very end of the age." (Matthew 28:20b)

Much later, I learned more about Duquesne University. Founded by a Catholic order called the Spiritans, its formal name is Duquesne University of the Holy Spirit. What a wonderful place to experience the presence of God that saved me and turned my life around!

Not about Donna

After my experience with the Lord in Pittsburgh, I returned to camp in the mountains. I wanted to share with Donna that I had read the five books in the Bible and become a Christian. I was hopeful that she would let me take her out on a date.

But I was surprised again. When I reached camp, I discovered that another instructor was lighting a camp stove and it blew up on him. He was burned and was soaking in a cool creek to deal with the pain.

Our group found him in the creek, helped him into a van, and drove him to a burn center. Donna learned of the leader's accident and nursed him back to health. Over the course of his recovery, love bloomed between the two of them. As a result, I never dated Donna.

What happened between Donna and me was not really about dating at all. It was about God using her to direct my steps so I would open the Bible and have my life completely transformed by the Word of God. Though I thought it was about Donna, in reality, it was about Jesus and me!

God Had Been Working in Me for a Long Time

As I came to Christ, I reflected on my life. I remembered several people and experiences that God used before I was a Christian to help me see him and to prepare me for that weekend in Pittsburgh. Like a roadmap, my story had been marked with names of people who had gently steered me toward God before I even knew him.

God had also worked in my life through:

- An older woman who led a Christian kids' club in my neighborhood when I was a boy.
- Dr. Reusch, an example of what God can do in a man's life, who led my confirmation training class when I was a teenager.
- Bushwhack Bill, an Outward Bound Instructor, who shared his faith openly and joyfully with me when I was in my twenties.

Throughout our lives, God moves in and around us to help us see him and receive his Son as our Savior and Lord. He is calling us to follow him.

God had the right plan for Donna, and he had the right plan for me. His plan for me was, through Donna's witness, to read those five books of the Bible. Through his life-giving Word and his Spirit, God got a hold of my heart.

Keeping the Discipline of Doing "Solos"

From that summer forward, I have loved walking with Jesus. As I have walked with him, I have found some ways that I connect with God and grow best. As a matter of fact, one of the ways God has deepened my understanding of myself and him best is through the solo.

Psalm 139:7–10 says:

⁷ *Where can I go from your Spirit?*
Where can I flee from your presence?
⁸ *If I go up to the heavens, you are there;*
if I make my bed in the depths, you are there.
⁹ *If I rise on the wings of the dawn,*
if I settle on the far side of the sea,
¹⁰ *even there your hand will guide me,*
your right hand will hold me fast."

When I became a Christian, I realized that God is everywhere. When I do a "solo" in the wilderness, God is there.

I have found that, by getting away from everyday life for three days and two nights, I can turn down the volume of the mundane and turn up the volume of the holy. This inspired my three-day and two-night "prayer retreat" experiences in which I seek the Lord and ask for his guidance. Over the past forty years, most of the major decisions I have made in ministry and life have come during prayer retreats. I share more about this life-changing spiritual discipline in some of my other books.

Perhaps you need to get away. In the decade of life known as your twenties, you are responsible for making some major decisions that will shape the course of the rest of your life. Where will you live? What will you do for a living? Whom will you date? How will you spend your money? How will you pay off student loans? What will your hobbies and priorities be?

It can be the same in other seasons of life and change as well. Maybe you are facing a job change or a move. Maybe you are facing a change of roles in an organization or a new project that needs God's direction. Whatever major decisions you're making, they require major prayer. That's why I believe getting away for three-day, two-night prayer retreats is absolutely pivotal. They give you an opportunity to hear from God clearly so you can step forward confidently.

If you do not have that much time to give, choose an afternoon or a day away. By getting alone and getting quiet with your Bible and God, you may hear some of the clearest guidance you need for the season that's coming next in your life. It could be a "solo" that changes everything!

LIFE LESSONS

- Getting away from the world for a little while can bring clarity, self-awareness, maturity, and even life-change.
- Wherever you go, God is there! See Psalm 139:8–10.
- If you are a Christian, choose not to date nonbelievers. You can hold your ground and encourage people to pursue the Lord before they get to be in a dating relationship with you. See 2 Corinthians 6:14.
- God's Word has power! Unlike any other word from anyone on earth, God's Word changes people from the inside out. Make reading his Word a daily priority in your life. See Isaiah 55:11.

WHAT ABOUT YOU?

1. Have you ever spent an extended period of time away from others so you could think, journal, pray, or reflect? What did you realize or learn during that time? When can you get away again?

2. Do you believe that Donna had a good principle in mind when she told me that because she believed in Jesus she didn't go out with unbelievers? Why or why not? (You might want to check out 2 Corinthians 6:14 before answering this question.)

3. How did the Lord lead you to place your trust in Jesus? Have you written down your story? Can you tell your story in five minutes to help someone who doesn't yet know Christ to see how the Lord worked in your life? Take a minute to practice writing it out.

4. Can you tell the Jesus story in five minutes? For tools to help you tell others about Jesus, visit Navigators.org and look for "Resources."

5. If you haven't yet made your commitment to Christ, would you consider taking a few days alone to read the first five books of the New Testament? God may reveal himself to you as he did to me.

9

JESUS WANTS TO WORK THROUGH YOUR LIFE IN POWER!

"The truth is that God can do anything He pleases through an ordinary person who is fully dedicated to Him."

–HENRY T. BLACKABY, CHURCH PLANTER

In adventure, it is easy to flip from confident to petrified in a matter of seconds. Things change quickly in the wilderness, and people who seem nearly unshakeable can find themselves bawling their eyes out at the impossibility and bigness of nature around them. God's creation has an ability to break you, humble you, and make you realize that you need God.

Concrete civilization can create a false sense of security and self-reliance, which I have noticed fades the minute people encounter the challenges of the wilderness.

I witnessed this firsthand during the summer of 1977. I was still leading adventures with Outward Bound. As before, my job was to help teenagers who were in a youth prison.

That summer, I met a teen named Kevin. Kevin came from the slums of Philadelphia. He was the strongest kid I'd met in a while. He had a gentle nature, but he was built like a bodybuilder. He had massive, chiseled muscles, and he looked like he could become a professional football player. Once, Kevin took his shirt off while our team was doing a ropes course, and I thought, *Those muscles are incredible!* This kid was huge. That summer, as I spent time with Kevin, we talked about what Jesus did in my life during my weekend reading the Bible in a dorm room in Pittsburgh. We talked about giving my life to Christ.

Broken by the Mountain

One warm Pennsylvania day, our team of two instructors and eight students hiked into the Allegheny Mountains. It was gorgeous that day. We walked through a forest of evergreens, where pine, spruce, and fir trees lined the trail. We passed through groves of birch, ash, maple, and oak. The rich smells of nature whirled around us, captivating our senses better than any big-screen movie. The earthy scent of the leaves rising from the forest floor just worshipped God as a truly wonderful creator. I was happy to be a follower of Jesus, and I spoke openly about Jesus to Kevin.

Into the mountains we went. The Allegheny Mountains lie on a bedrock of sandstone and quartzite. As we rounded a corner, I saw a sixty-foot vertical quartzite cliff. A person could easily walk around it from the bottom to the top, making it great for instructing students in rappelling. We set ourselves up with Bob, the other instructor, at the top of the cliff with the team and me at the bottom to help the young climbers get unclipped from the rope. Bob secured the rappelling rope and the belay rope to a boulder at the top while the students got into their harnesses.

I heard the first climber call "On rappel" at the top. That climber leaned out and over the cliff. Just as I had on my first rappel, the climber put his feet flat up against the rock face and leaned his weight back over the edge. He walked and bounced his way to the bottom as the rope let him down. When his feet hit the ground, I unhooked him, and he walked back up to the top to be with the rest of the team. Climber after climber came down the rappel rope until seven of the eight had completed the descent. The last student left was Kevin.

I knew Kevin was getting connected to the belay rope and to the rappel rope. I heard the instructor at the top yell, "On belay!" I looked up the cliff. Kevin was being instructed to lean back. He did…a little. Then he moved back into standing position on the edge of the cliff. Two more times, the instructor encouraged him to "lean back and trust the rope." Two more times, Kevin leaned back a little and then popped back into a standing position on the edge. The instructor on top called down to me and said, "Paul, we're going to take Kevin off the rope."

I hurried around the cliff and up the path to the top. When I got there, I saw Kevin sitting by himself, crying. Fear of the sixty-foot cliff had broken him. Immediately I worried about him, first because he couldn't do the rappel. Even worse, I was worried about the response of the other students around him. He was crying in the presence of tough juvenile delinquents from the slums. Showing weakness with these kids would set the stage for relentless bullying in the future. I was anxious that they would gang up on him and humiliate him for showing weakness.

I sat beside Kevin on the leafy ground. He wept as he told me, "I can't do it. I just can't do it. I'm scared." I watched as he became quiet.

Then I spoke. "Kevin, you know that the ropes will hold you." I shared the comforting words of my own rappelling instructor: "A climbing rope can hold a Volkswagen without breaking. It can hold you."

Through his tears, Kevin said, "I know it will hold me, but I'm just scared. I lean back, and then the fear comes, and suddenly I know I just can't do it."

"Kevin, you know, my first rappel was my hardest. It was only a twenty-foot rappel, but I was just terrified. I looked down, and I couldn't do it. But my friend, my instructor, helped me, and finally, I did it. It was a wonderful feeling, overcoming that fear. Would it help you if I were the belayer?"

"Yeah, I'd like that," Kevin replied. "That would be better."

"Okay, let's try again," I encouraged.

Still in his climbing harness, Kevin got hooked up to the belay rope. Then I connected him to a figure-eight belay/rappel device and put the second rope through that device so he could slide down it to the bottom. The other instructor went to the bottom to help Kevin arrive safely. I got connected to the anchor at the top and wrapped the belay rope around my waist.

I called out, "On belay," and fed the rope out a little.

Kevin said, "On rappel!" and he leaned back. He looked down. His eyes caught mine as they got big and filled with fear. He bounced back up to a standing position on top of the cliff.

"One more time," I said. "On belay."

Again, he called out, "On rappel!" He leaned back, looked down, became terrified, and popped back up.

Tears rolled down his dark, strong cheeks. "I want off this rope. I just can't do it. I'm too afraid!"

I said, "Just give me one more time. Okay, Kevin? When you lean back, you look down. That's what has you so frightened. You're looking at a sixty-foot drop, and you're afraid you are going to fall. This time, I don't want you to look down. Look at me."

Who's Got You?

"We're going to do it this time. Kevin, you're on belay!" I explained as I tightened the belay rope around my waist.

Without much conviction, Kevin said, "On rappel," and started to lean back.

"Kevin, do not look down. I want you to look right at me." I began to let out the rope just a little. Still, I made sure that he could feel that I had tension on the rope, that I had his weight.

He tried to look down.

"Don't do it, Kevin! Look at me. Look right in my eyes. You're not going to fall. I won't let you fall. I have you, Kevin."

Kevin was leaning back. He was looking in my eyes. Suddenly, a big smile came across his face. He said, "I know you have me, Paul. Jesus has me too, doesn't he?!"

I said, "Yes, Jesus has you. He won't let you fall!"

Kevin took his first step down the cliff, and a miracle happened right before our eyes. Those students, those tough young guys who had committed crimes like armed robbery and assault and attempted murder, began to clap and call out their encouragement to Kevin. Once he got started, Kevin went all the way down the cliff like a champ. He unhooked at the bottom, and I got out of my belay position at the top.

Before I could go down to congratulate him, a deep, joyful gratitude welled up inside me as I realized God had just moved in power. I walked away by myself into the bushes and began to weep. For the first time, I had just experienced God work through me to touch other lives in a powerful way. The presence of Jesus had filled Kevin with courage, and it had touched this whole group of tough guys.

I realized that Jesus was with me. But more than that, Jesus wasn't just someone *I* needed. He was for me, yes. But Jesus was for others, too. Tough guys like Kevin needed him, too. In those moments at the top of the cliff, when Kevin needed him the most, Jesus was with Kevin. And then, through Kevin's example of trust, Jesus changed the group of tough guys.

For the first time, I thought, *Jesus is meant for sharing. Jesus is with me. Jesus is with them, too!*

Keeping Our Eyes on Jesus

In the middle of the mountains of Pennsylvania, I encountered Jesus' realness so powerfully that he not only touched my heart but emboldened a timid tough guy and transformed a troop of aggressive teens into encouragers. This is one of the reasons I both respect and love adventure. When people go out into God's creation, they are confronted with their smallness and God's bigness.

People are meant to realize they are small in contrast to God. We were made by a God so big that he spoke and the entire universe came into existence. He is big and mighty, and we can run to him anytime with any need. When we fortify ourselves with the comforts and concrete of civilization, we forfeit the understanding that we need God. We miss out on the overwhelming blessing that comes from trusting in him in our time of need.

As the hymn writer Annie Sherwood Hawks so wonderfully put it:
I need thee every hour,
most gracious Lord;
no tender voice like thine
can peace afford.
I need thee, O I need thee;

every hour I need thee;
O bless me now, my Savior,
I come to thee.

Annie Sherwood Hawks understood something so profound that it took me years of nature adventures to realize: when people know they need God, they receive the amazing blessing of his peace and presence, and they receive the provision they need from God.

Kevin needed courage. As he fixed his eyes on me, he realized Jesus gave him that courage.

What is it in your life that you need right now? What would it look like for you to fix your eyes on Jesus as you wait for his peace, presence, and provision to meet that need?

In my life of following Jesus, and in my leadership of four new churches and at Dynamic Church Planting International, I have encountered many, many times of need. In my first church, after a powerful launch, I lost the support of my steering committee. They no longer wanted me as their leader. I didn't know if I would be allowed to continue pastoring that church. I was deeply in need of help and so was the church. God provided for me, my family, and the church in the best way possible. You will have to read my next book for the rest of the story.

When God's people encounter experiences, tasks, and adventures that take us beyond our abilities, the best response is to keep our eyes on Jesus. He is holding you, like a good belayer holds the rappeller. Just as Kevin kept his eyes on mine instead of looking over the edge of the cliff, we are to keep our eyes on Jesus without focusing our attention on the fear of the daunting tasks before us.

Jesus said, "Come to me, all you who are weary and burdened, and
I will give you rest. Take my yoke upon you and learn from me,

for I am gentle and humble in heart, and you will find rest for your souls. For my yoke is easy and my burden is light" (Matthew 11:28–30).

When God places challenges in your path, he never expects you to face them alone. When you feel weary and burdened, like you just can't do it, God does not expect you to go the road alone.

Just as Kevin would not have been able to rappel safely by himself, God doesn't expect us to press forward without his faithful, loving presence. He is the one holding our lives.

The Bible says, "Blessed are the meek, for they shall inherit the earth" (Matthew 5:5).

Meekness is a quiet, humble knowledge that you need God and can trust him to work. That is why our call as Christians is not a call to power but to meekness. It's okay to be in need. In fact, it's a good thing. It reminds you of who is in charge of the world, anyway. It's okay to be unable. It reminds us of the One who is able! It's okay to be stuck. It reminds us of the Way Maker!

So, if you have felt in need, weak, or stuck recently, I encourage you. Those circumstances are opening your eyes to a God who is strong and mighty, who is always with you, who holds every moment of your life, and who is working something powerful in the current season of your life. He can do exceedingly, abundantly more than you can ask or imagine.

Remember, Ephesians 3:20–21 says, "Now to him who is able to do immeasurably more than all we ask or imagine, according to his power that is at work within us, to him be glory in the church and in Christ Jesus throughout all generations, for ever and ever! Amen."

With eyes fixed on Jesus, we can take our burdens to him and find that he will give us his peace, presence, and provision as we whisper in the quiet places of our souls, "I need thee. O I need thee. Every hour I need thee. O bless me now, my Savior. I come to thee."

When you come to the Savior to meet your need, just watch what God will do in you and through you.

Immeasurably more than all you can ask or imagine!

LIFE LESSONS

- Jesus is for you, and he is for those around you! Talk openly about him because others need him just as much as you do, even if they don't know it yet. See Romans 5:8.
- Keep your eyes on Jesus. Focusing on circumstances can be overwhelming, but focusing on Jesus keeps you steady and secure, no matter what you face. See John 16:33.
- Knowing you need God is an invitation for him to give you his peace, presence, and provision.
- God wants to move through your life in power. See Ephesians 3:20.
- Jesus is meant for sharing! See Mark 16:15.

WHAT ABOUT YOU?

1. Whom would you like to introduce to Jesus?
2. What does this passage of Scripture mean to you? "But in your hearts revere Christ as Lord. Always be prepared to give an answer to everyone who asks you to give the reason for the hope that you have. But do this with gentleness and respect." (1 Peter 3:15)
3. Recognizing who God has made you to be, how can you most effectively share Jesus with those people?
4. Have you felt unable, stuck, or in need lately? How has that pointed you back to the God who can do immeasurably more than you ask or imagine (Ephesians 3:20–21)?

10

JUMPING OFF HAWKSBILL MOUNTAIN

> *"As an adventurer...I try to protect against the downside.*
> *I make sure I have covered as many eventualities as I can.*
> *In the end, you have to take calculated risks; otherwise*
> *you're going to sit in mothballs all day and do nothing."*
>
> **–SIR RICHARD BRANSON**

> *"I want to take the calculated risk;*
> *to dream and to build, to fail and to succeed."*
>
> **–DEAN ALFANGE**

"Are you kidding me? There is no way I am jumping off this mountain! That's suicide!" said my friend, the experienced rock-climbing instructor from Arizona.

This jump really did look like it would lead to certain death. None of us were sure this was a good idea. But part of our ongoing training as Outward Bound Instructors was to attend Outward Bound School in North Carolina in the United States, where we would sharpen our skills, receive continuing education in our outdoor work, and jump off of Hawksbill Mountain.

Now mind you, I was quite used to high-intensity adrenaline rushes at this point in my life. I had led groups of students to do the wildest things in the Rocky Mountains in Colorado. I had led excursions where we paddled through thousands of lakes in the Boundary Waters Wilderness of Minnesota and carried our canoes overhead on land bridges. I had led groups of young people along the C & O Canal and rock climbing in the same state park where the presidential retreat, Camp David, is located. At my college, I had launched the NATURE program, in which we canoed the Everglades at night and practiced our survival skills on a deserted island off the coast of west Florida. For days, we hiked through the rain in the Smoky Mountains, and we had our rafts blow across the Colorado River. All of these wildly unforgettable experiences made me love the rush of energy and endorphins I felt when trying something new and a bit scary. I loved playing with a new skill and seeing an unfamiliar stunning view. But truly, nothing I did as an Outward Bound Instructor scared me more than what we were asked to do on Hawksbill Mountain.

Heading up Hawksbill

One warm morning in June of 1967, a group of other instructors and I hiked to the top of Hawksbill Mountain. It is not the tallest mountain in North Carolina, measuring only 4,050 feet in height. At the top, however, is a rock that looks like a hawk's bill that juts out into space with nothing underneath it but air. This is where my stomach started to get a little unsettled.

Without telling us the full extent of the adventure, our guides hiked us up to the top of Hawksbill Mountain. When we got there, one of my teammates asked, "Okay, we're here. Now what?"

Jim, the Master Trainer, said, "As part of your ongoing education, you are all going to jump off Hawksbill Mountain...with your rappelling gear, of course." Then he laughed.

Not funny! I thought.

I walked over to the edge of the hawk's bill and looked down. Remember, I don't like heights. They scare me. Even watching a TV show in which someone is dangling over a building gives me a fearful, sick, dizzy feeling in my stomach. Looking out over Hawksbill Mountain made my spine straighten, my palms sweat, and my breath get really shallow. Beneath the hawk's bill, the mountain was undercut for one hundred feet. That means we would have to do a free rappel. Our feet wouldn't be on the rock. Then, after the initial one hundred feet, we would have another one hundred feet of standard rappelling down the rest of the rock. That meant this rappel was two hundred feet tall. That is a *long* rappel.

At this point in my adventuring career, I was comfortable rappelling down a rock face, but a free descent, hanging from a rope, spinning in midair with nothing touching my boots, made me want to vomit.

What most spiked my fear, however, was the fact that you could see two thousand feet down into the Linville Gorge. If you fell, you would actually fall only two hundred feet, which is the same height as a twenty-story building—still high enough to kill a person easily! But the perceived fall was two thousand feet down into the gorge below. That is what your mind sees.

More of the instructors were joining me at the edge now. A couple of them were laughing hysterically due to the fear. Some of them were just shaking their heads back and forth as if to say, "No. No. No. This is nonsense."

That's when Jim, the Master Trainer, dropped the big truth bomb. He said, "You guys noticed there is nowhere to put your feet when you begin this rappel. That means you're going to rope up, sit on the very edge with your legs dangling over, take up about ten feet of slack in the rope, and then fall off Hawksbill Mountain in your rappel arrest position."

Rappel arrest position is a way of holding the rope so that you catch yourself and come to a stop. That meant we would fall about ten feet off the mountain, then come to a sudden stop. Did you notice that? We start by freefalling off the mountain!

The gasp could be heard in the mountaintops.

One of my peers said, "There's no way I'm going to do this rappel. This is just nuts."

Another one of us said, "I've been rock climbing and rappelling for fifteen years. I've never been faced with a rappel like this, and I'm not going to start now."

I wanted to say, "I'm going back the way we came up. I'll meet you guys at the bottom," but I held my tongue and just walked away from the group.

My mind flashed to a scene from an old movie I watched as a kid called *Butch Cassidy and the Sundance Kid*. The two men are being chased and have a quick conversation before jumping over a cliff. It goes something like this:

Butch Cassidy: All right, I'll jump first.

Sundance Kid: No.

Butch Cassidy: Then you jump first.

Sundance Kid: No, I said.

Butch Cassidy: What's the matter with you?

Sundance Kid: I can't swim.

Butch Cassidy: Are you crazy? The fall will probably kill you.

"The fall will probably kill you" echoed through my mind. What was I going to do—bail out like these guys or go for it?

Scared to death, I tried to reason with myself. *Let's look at the facts. I will be hooked up to a climbing rope that has a tensile strength of five thousand pounds. That rope can lift a rhinoceros into the air without breaking. I can trust the Master Trainer. They've done this rappel for years and no one has died—that I know about. I'm pretty strong and should be able to hold my rappel arrest position even after falling ten feet.*

I considered all my options, and all I could come up with was *I think I can, I think I can*, and *Let's get this over with.*

I walked back to the group, and soon it was my turn. The Master Trainer made sure I was attached securely to the rappel rope. I had my eight-ring belay/rappel device with the climbing rope through it. The rappel rope was wrapped around my waist and held tight by my right hand against my stomach. *Go time*, I thought. I sat on the very tip of the hawk's bill, holding ten feet of rope in my lap.

Jim, the Master Trainer, called out, "On belay!"

I called out, "On rappel!"

And then…I slid my hips forward and jumped face-first off Hawksbill Mountain!

It seemed to take forever before the rope stopped me, but it was probably only a second. I could hear my heart beating in my ears, and my sweaty palms clung tightly to the rope around my waist. There is some spring to a climbing rope, so I was able to keep my grip. Suddenly, I found myself hanging ten feet below the hawk's bill, just bobbing away. I was so relieved I let out a "Whoop!"

Then I let out a little slack and began sliding down the rope and twirling around. It was strange not being able to put my feet on anything, but I was too far away from the cliff. What a great way to have a wonderful view of the cliff and Linville Gorge below. Now that

I had taken the leap, I was strangely calm and very happy. I was now about one hundred feet below the hawk's bill and could place my feet on the rock and lean back. It became a regular rappel the rest of the way.

This felt like a real accomplishment. I had faced one of my worst fears—the fear of heights—and, in an extremely frightening environment, took a calculated risk and succeeded in the rappel.

Facing Fears

Whew! What a rush of pride and satisfaction I felt after facing my fear! Did you know that fear of heights is actually the third most common fear people have? I wasn't alone in dreading this experience. The other top ten fears include fear of flying, fear of public speaking, fear of the dark, fear of intimacy, fear of death, fear of failure, fear of rejection, fear of spiders, and fear of commitment.

That's the thing about fear, though. When you are in a relationship with God, your fears have a place to hide.

Psalm 91:1 says, "Whoever dwells in the shelter of the Most High will rest in the shadow of the Almighty."

When you're in a relationship with God, you are so close to him that it's like you're hiding in his shadow. Your fears are safe and sound in the shadow of God.

Proverbs 18:10 says, "The name of the LORD is a fortified tower; the righteous run to it and are safe."

God is your shelter. He is your hiding place. He is the One who enables you to do things beyond your capacity and outside your comfort zone. At any moment of any day, in the middle of your greatest fears, you can pray quietly in your heart and find security in God who is your Strong Tower! When you pray amidst your fears, you run into a strong fortress like a warrior in the middle of a battle, and there inside, you get to rest.

Psalm 56:3 says, "When I am afraid, I put my trust in you."

When your hands are shaking and your fears are overwhelming, you can place them in the steady hands of the God who holds the whole universe! When you are afraid of the future, afraid of that project, afraid of taking that trip or making that call, afraid of giving up something that God is calling you to give up, afraid of going through something again that was really hard the first time, afraid of taking that leap of faith, you can put your trust in him. His hands are steady. He keeps you safe. He holds your life. He knows every moment before any of them happen.

To live with these fears is to miss out on the amazing life God has planned for you. Fear of flying can keep us from seeing the world. Fear of public speaking can keep us from ever getting up in front of a crowd and sharing the powerful testimony we've been given. Fear of intimacy can keep us from building strong, lasting, deep relationships with others. Fears will limit your life, but God wants to take you beyond your wildest dreams, if you'll place your fears in his hands.

Calculated Risks

When you are confronted by a fearful situation, try to calculate your risk. In Outward Bound, we tried to confront people with significant challenges that looked death-defying but actually were very safe. In life, there's a difference between taking insane risks and taking calculated risks. Before jumping off Hawksbill Mountain, I calculated my risk. I assessed the situation, and I decided that it would be safe. When I was diving in the cave (in chapter one), I took too many risks that were real risks of death. In fact, had my buddy not saved me in the nick of time, I almost certainly would have died 120 feet down inside that underwater tunnel. I hadn't calculated any risks, which is why I took so many stupid steps toward my almost-death.

What is the calculated risk that you need to jump into now? Maybe for you it's a new job, a new school, a new living situation, or even a new city to live in. Maybe it's a new ministry or a new giving opportunity. Maybe it's a trip or adventure you need to go on. Calculate it, then leap into a calculated risk! To quote almost every Outward Bound Instructor: "You Can Do It!"

LIFE LESSON

- God wants to take you beyond your wildest dreams, if you'll place your fears in his hands! See Psalm 56:3.
- When you take calculated risks led by the Holy Spirit, you get to reap the reward of participating in the amazing things God is doing in this world. See Ephesians 2:10.

WHAT ABOUT YOU?

1. What are your greatest fears?
2. What do you think God would say to you about those fears?
3. What fear do you want to overcome in your life? What step toward overcoming that fear will you take today?
4. Remember, "I can do all this through him who gives me strength" (Philippians 4:13). Substitute your name for the "I" in this verse. Say it out loud. Claim the power in this Bible verse to help you overcome.

EPILOGUE

THE ADVENTURE CONTINUES

"We are made in the image of God; we carry within us the desire for our true life of intimacy and adventure."

–JOHN ELDREDGE

"For it is God who works in you to will and to act in order to fulfill his good purpose."

–PHILIPPIANS 2:13

Writing here in Steamboat Springs, Colorado, almost fifty years after many of the adventures in this book happened, I can still feel the exhilaration and wonder of these events so close to my heart.

As I look back on what has happened in my life during the last half century, I think of the book of Acts in the Bible. Some call this book the

Acts of the Apostles. Personally, I think the book should be considered the Acts of the Holy Spirit *through* the apostles and ordinary people like you and me. In Acts, as in my life, God gets all the glory for what he has done and will do.

What you have just read is the first book of leadership and life lessons that flow from my experiences while walking on the wild side with God. Those early years were exciting and unbridled, and I cherish their memories. As I grew, God continued leading me to new, wild, and stunning adventures that blew my mind and shattered my entire perception of what my grown-up life would look like.

In the Second Book

In the second book, I will bring you ten stories of how the Lord led me in my late twenties and thirties, and how he used that time to guide me into the future version of myself.

You'll hear about twenty-six-year-old me, who hitchhiked across the United States to Central Oregon and met the wisest man I'd ever met when he picked me up in the Warm Springs Indian Reservation. You'll hear how I decided to stay and learn the Word of God and life lessons from him, and received great love and acceptance from his church. You will hear how I met my late wife through him and started serving the Lord under his loving leadership. You'll hear how God laid foundational habits in my life so that I could listen to God.

You'll also hear about how my first wife and I moved to San Diego, California, had two kids, started a church, and then started three more churches. The adventures of church planting were more challenging than Outward Bound! I am so proud of our two children, Jessica and Brandon, for how they participated in the work God did in those days and for how they continue to serve the Lord to this day.

You'll hear about how God led us to start helping other pastors plant churches to reach precious people for Christ. Then, the story of the tragedy and rebirth that came into our lives. You will read about my first wife being diagnosed with breast cancer. During the decade of the 1990s until her death in 1999, that cancer battle marked me and our two children with loss and desolation, but it didn't stop us from following the Lord and serving him.

In the Third Book

In the third book, you'll hear about the ways in which the Lord led me from the mid-1990s through this year. In 1994, the Lord gave me a vision as I climbed Stonewall Peak in eastern San Diego County: "Start a new nonprofit ministry that is dedicated solely to equipping church-planting leaders worldwide."

That ministry became Dynamic Church Planting International (DCPI).

This is the story of visiting more than one hundred countries as God built his network of church-planting leaders to fulfill his vision to plant five million dynamic churches to reach every country of the world.

In 2000, the Lord sent me a great gift. Her name is Cathy, and she became my second wife. She has been an incredible gift to my children and to our mission. I prayed for a wife who would serve full-time in our mission, and the Lord answered that prayer far beyond all my expectations in Cathy. In recent years, the Lord gave us incredible grandparent joy when our granddaughter, Lynnlee, and then grandson, Joshua Paul, were born.

I have served as president and founder of DCPI for twenty-six years. It has been a wild ride, seeing what God can do! I can't wait to tell you about it in the third book.

The Story of DCPI

Here's a sneak peek: as of September 2020, the Lord has worked through our DCPI trained leaders to plant more than 830,000 churches in 159 nations of the world. Praise God from whom all blessings flow!

The story of Dynamic Church Planting International is the story of God giving four visions to our mission and then fulfilling these visions. The Birth of a Mission in 1994. The Million Church Vision in 1997. The "Every Country" Vision in 2004. And the Five Million Church Vision in 2009. We are now on the verge of seeing God finish the Million Church Vision. As God fulfills the Five Million Church Vision, he will double the number of churches on the planet!

The story of Dynamic Church Planting International is really the story of incredible apostolic visionary leaders from all around the world. God has moved them to adopt the Five Million Church Vision. It is all about the vision!

It is the story of a boy born a Hindu in an untouchable village in India, who becomes one of the greatest church-planting movement leaders in the world.

It is the story of another village boy in Kenya who yearns to serve the Lord and earns his PhD in leadership development from a world-class seminary in the United States. He returns home to plant a huge church in Nairobi and train tens of thousands of church planters in more than fifteen countries, including Pakistan and Great Britain.

It is the story of tens of thousands of other church-planting leaders who are actively training leaders to plant the five million dynamic churches.

Read the third book in this trilogy to hear incredible stories of leaders who are walking on the wild side with God in their countries and the world.

These books are really all about God and you. These books are meant to inspire you with the incredible work that God wants to do in and through you in your life, if you are willing to "walk on the wild side" with him!

LIFE LESSON

- God will do great things through your life if you "walk on the wild side" of faith in him. See Luke 1:37.

WHAT ABOUT YOU?

1. What are some things God taught you through this book?

2. In what ways is God calling you to live by faith right now?

3. List some people, experiences, or adventures that God has used to shape your life so far. How do you think each of these impacted you?

4. What is one Bible verse that stood out to you in this book? Memorize it!

5. What is your prayer for your next phase of life?

ABOUT THE AUTHORS

Paul Becker is the President and Founder of Dynamic Church Planting International (DCPI). He is a prayerful, focused, visionary leader called by God to equip and multiply indigenous visionary leaders to fulfill DCPI's Five Million Church Vision. He has planted four churches, authored five books on church planting, and mentored hundreds of leaders in church planting. The amazing worldwide team of DCPI has trained more than 325,000 leaders to establish churches in 162 countries. According to best research, we project these leaders have planted more than 863,000 churches that are reaching more than 38 million precious people for Christ. He and his wife, Cathy, serve together in DCPI's mission. One of their joys is to spend time with their children and two grandchildren. Paul loves the mountains. He has stood on the peak of Mount Kilimanjaro.

Amy Bayer is the Director of Recruitment and Retention at DCPI as well as a marketing consultant and copywriter, specializing in working with small businesses and nonprofits in the United States. She is a follower of Jesus who enjoys adventuring and healthy cooking with her husband and four young children. Amy is passionate about reaching the world for Jesus Christ, and she has made it her mission to help leaders communicate their thoughts and stories clearly. She holds an MS in integrated marketing communications from West Virginia University and a BS in international business from Biola University.

Books Already Published

Dynamic Church Planting: A Complete Handbook by Paul Becker

The Dynamic Daughter Church Planting Handbook by Mark Williams and Paul Becker

The New Dynamic Church Planting Handbook by Paul Becker, Jim Carpenter and Mark Williams

Seeing Your Vision Come True by Paul Becker

How to Experience an Effective Personal Prayer Retreat by Paul Becker

Books Coming Soon

Coming Soon: *Walk on the Wild Side with God* is the first in a three-part series about living by faith and enjoying big adventures with God. Two more books like this one will be coming out in the next couple years that tell the rest of the story of what God did in Paul Becker's life through church planting, the death of a spouse, starting an international missions organization, and more.

CPSIA information can be obtained
at www.ICGtesting.com
Printed in the USA
BVHW072040060721
611232BV00011B/1227